DANCE IMPROVISATIONS

Warm-Ups, Games and Choreographic Tasks

Justine Reeve, BA, PGCE, PGDip

Human Kinetics

Library of Congress Cataloging-in-Publication Data

Reeve, Justine.
  Dance improvisations : warm-ups, games and choreographic tasks / Justine Reeve.
    p. cm.
  ISBN-13: 978-1-4504-0214-9 (soft cover)
  ISBN-10: 1-4504-0214-3 (soft cover)
  1. Improvisation in dance.   I. Title.
  GV1781.2.R44 2011
  792.8--dc22

                                                          2010053614

ISBN-10: 1-4504-0214-3 (print)
ISBN-13: 978-1-4504-0214-9 (print)

Acquisitions Editor: Gayle Kassing, PhD; **Developmental Editor:** Melissa Feld; **Assistant Editor:** Rachel Brito; **Copyeditor:** Joanna Hatzopoulos; **Permission Manager:** Dalene Reeder; **Graphic Designer:** Fred Starbird; **Graphic Artists:** Dawn Sills and Yvonne Griffith; **Cover Designer:** Keith Blomberg; **Photographer (cover and interior):** All photos courtesy of Caitlin Reeve, except photo on page 171 by Andy Cloke; **Photo Production Manager:** Jason Allen; **Printer:** Versa Press

Printed in the United States of America   10 9 8 7 6 5 4 3 2 1

The paper in this book is certified under a sustainable forestry program.

Human Kinetics
Website: www.HumanKinetics.com

United States: Human Kinetics
P.O. Box 5076
Champaign, IL 61825-5076
800-747-4457
e-mail: humank@hkusa.com

Canada: Human Kinetics
475 Devonshire Road Unit 100
Windsor, ON N8Y 2L5
800-465-7301 (in Canada only)
e-mail: info@hkcanada.com

Europe: Human Kinetics
107 Bradford Road
Stanningley
Leeds LS28 6AT, United Kingdom
+44 (0) 113 255 5665
e-mail: hk@hkeurope.com

Australia: Human Kinetics
57A Price Avenue
Lower Mitcham, South Australia 5062
08 8372 0999
e-mail: info@hkaustralia.com

New Zealand: Human Kinetics
PO Box 80
Torrens Park, South Australia 5062
0800 222 062
e-mail: info@hknewzealand.com

E5304

Contents

Improvisation Finder

Improvisation name	Page number	Organisational pattern	Approximate duration	Level of difficulty
Accumulation Nation	87	Whole group	5–20 min	Moderate
Body Actions	104	Whole group, solo task	5–15 min	Moderate
Body Part Conversation	106	Partners	5–20 min	Complex
Cat and Mouse	15	Partners and whole group	5–10 min	Easy
Chase the Mouse	27	Whole group in rows	5–10 min	Easy
Circle Dircle	52	Circle	5 min	Easy
Circle of Trust	126	Whole group	10 min	Moderate
Clay Sculpting	124	Partners	10–20 min	Moderate/ Complex
The Connection	120	Partners	5–15 min	Moderate
Counterbalance	134	Partners	15–30 min	Complex
Crowd Surfing	139	Whole group	10 min	Complex
Cup of Tea	19	Whole group roaming	5 min	Easy
Different Quadrants	48	Whole group roaming	5–10 min	Easy
Disjointed	80	Whole group, solo task	5– 20 min	Complex
Elastic Force	85	Whole group and pair work	5–20 min	Complex
Encounters	116	Whole group, half groups	5–15 min	Moderate
Energy Impulses	78	Partners	5–20 min	Complex
Falling	141	Partners	10 min	Complex
Fill the Space	154	Partners	10–20 min	Moderate
Find Five Lifts	137	Partners	15–30 min	Complex

Improvisation name	Page number	Organisational pattern	Approximate duration	Level of difficulty
Five Curves	50	Whole group, solo task	5–15 min	Moderate
Five Seconds	38	Circle	5 min	Easy
Focus Up	29	Circle	5 min	Easy
Follow You, Follow Me	23	Whole group roaming	5–15 min	Easy
Forty-Five Degrees	114	Whole group, solo task	5–15 min	Complex
Four in One	17	Partners	5–10 min	Easy
Get Knotted	21	Whole group together	5–15 min	Easy
Ghost	156	On own	10–15 min	Complex
Greeting and Parting	36	Partners	5–10 min	Easy
Hospital Tag	31	Whole group roaming	5–10 min	Easy
How Many Body Parts?	54	Whole group roaming	5–10 min	Moderate
Intention Invention	163	On own and with partners	15–30 min	Complex
Introduce the Space	56	Whole group roaming	5–10 min	Moderate
Jelly Bubble	145	Groups of 3	15 min	Complex
The Journey	89	Whole group, solo task	5–20 min	Moderate
Jumping Jacks	91	Whole group, solo task	5–15 min	Moderate
Just Plain Running	64	Whole group roaming	5–10 min	Moderate
Keep the Awareness	143	Partners	10 min	Moderate
Keep the Shape	72	Whole group, smaller groups	5–10 min	Moderate
Lava Lamp	122	Partners	5–15 min	Moderate
Mirror or Follow	60	Partners	5–15 min	Easy

(continued)

Improvisation name	Page number	Organisational pattern	Approximate duration	Level of difficulty
Offer a Platform	130	Partners	10–20 min	Complex
Oiling the Joints	42	Whole group	5–10 min	Moderate
Paint the Space	76	Circle	5–20 min	Moderate
Palms	128	Partners	10 min	Moderate
Parts, Not the Whole	148	Small groups	15–30 min	Complex
Pass the Movement	58	Circle	5–10 min	Moderate
Puppet Strings	108	Whole group, pair work	5–20 min	Moderate
RADS and Restrictions	150	Partners and on own	15–30 min	Complex
A Recipe	165	On own, then with partners, then small groups	30–45 min	Complex
Restrictions	102	Whole group, solo task	5–20 min	Complex
Retiré	110	Whole group, solo task	5–10 min	Easy
Retrograde	161	On own	10 min	Complex
Rhythm Do	112	Whole group, solo task	5–20 min	Moderate
Rhythm Is a Dancer	94	Small groups	5–15 min	Moderate
Rhythm Nation	96	Whole group, solo task	5–10 min	Moderate
Same but Different	159	Partners	10–20 min	Complex
Sign In	70	Circle	5–10 min	Easy
Signal Circle	46	Circle	5-10 min	Moderate
Signals and Pulses	44	Whole group	5–10 min	Moderate
Space Race	98	Whole group, solo task	5–15 min	Moderate
Statues and Speed	62	Circle	5–10 min	Moderate
Swings and Suspension	40	Whole group, solo task	5–10 min	Moderate

Improvisation name	Page number	Organisational pattern	Approximate duration	Level of difficulty
Take Three Shapes	100	Whole group, solo task	5–15 min	Moderate
Taking Away	157	Partners, then on own	10–20 min	Complex
This Is Me	25	Circle	5–10 min	Easy
Time	82	Whole group, solo and pair work	5–20 min	Complex
Touch the Floor	66	Whole group roaming	5–10 min	Easy
Two Against One	132	Groups of 3	10 min	Complex
Who Started That?	33	Circle	5–10 min	Easy
Work, Work and All Play	68	Circle	5–15 min	Easy
Zoo Line	152	Small or large groups	15 min	Complex

Preface

Dance improvisation is a valuable tool for choreographers to use and an important skill for dancers to develop. A choreographer may use improvisation exercises to help generate movement material for new pieces. Improvisation allows a dancer to use the brain and body in concert in the creative process. Instead of following set choreography, the dancer relies on sensitivity to gravity, other dancers, other internal and external stimuli and momentum to create unique moments. Often these moments result in clever phrasing and innovative material that deeply affects an audience. Improvisation can be exciting for those performing it, too. Performing improvisation is like a dynamic chess game for the body and mind because each moment demands a movement response.

In a class or professional setting, improvisation exercises are useful warm-up activities. They get the heart rate up and warm up the body to safely dance. They also help dancers prepare in other ways. They can help to introduce a movement topic, to get used to a dance space or to get to know new teachers and peers.

This book can develop students' responses to different stimuli as well as challenge their understanding of choreography. Dancers can struggle with creativity; using improvisations in class and workshops can improve confidence and innovation. In improvisation much of the learning is based on the interactions and observations of peers.

This book contains dance improvisations to use as warm-ups, fun games and choreographic tasks that create innovative movement material for dancers at all levels. It is therefore every dance teacher's companion, whether you are teaching KS3, KS4 or Post 16 dance in schools or colleges. It will aid the student's creative responses to stimuli and can be used in nearly every lesson to warm dancers up. This book is ideal for teachers teaching GCSE, AS, A2 AQA Dance syllabi and EDEXCEL's BTEC Firsts and Nationals in dance performance and also the movement units on the acting and physical theatre principal subject areas. This book is also appropriate for teachers teaching middle school through college in the United States.

You do not have to be a dance teacher to lead a dance improvisation session. If you are a physical education teacher who has been thrown in at the deep end and are delivering dance with concerns about technical training, you can use this book to help your dancers create original movement that they can develop into choreography. It will also give you the right type of task for the expectations of exam boards that demand dancers be creative, innovative and original with sophisticated movement ideas. If there are any dance or choreographic terms used in the descriptions of each improvisation that are unknown, you will find an explanation in the glossary. You will also find the glossary useful when discussing the creations of your dancers as the terms can aid understanding, help to describe and evaluate creations as well as start to educate your creative dancers into being thoughtful and articulate dancers.

The improvisations in this book are ideal for a dance studio or similar space in school or college, but can also be used in drama classes and physical education spaces. In any space, adhere to all health and safety rules. For example, don't encourage dancers to jump on an unsprung floor, stretch in a cold space, dance around dangerous obstacles or lift each other if the ceiling is too low. Health and safety considerations are covered in chapter 1.

The book is divided into five clear sections to allow you to choose improvisations to create an innovative and fun session. Each improvisation has an introduction, a clear numbered list of activities, a teaching tip and suggestions for further development. You can quickly open a page on an improvisation that will work immediately in the classroom. To further save you time, there is an improvisation finder that will give you a quick guide to each improvisation including the organisational pattern, where to find it in the book and an idea of the duration and the level of difficulty. If you are looking for a quick and easy task for the whole group, you can thumb down the page to several improvisations that would fit this description.

Chapter 1 guides you through the improvisation experience. The first 10 improvisations in chapter 2 provide easy ways for newer teachers and dancers to access dance improvisation. Most of them are in a game format. This is a good way to introduce spontaneity because a movement choice must be made quickly in order for the game to continue. This fun way of playing is really behind all the improvisations in the book. Chapter 3 has movement investigations to help dancers extend the idea of play into creating new movements. It uses some fundamental ideas such as developing confidence in performance (as in Five Seconds, page 38) and how the body moves as a whole and in parts (as in Sign In, page 70). These skills are further developed in chapter 4 with improvisations that explore the use of time, force and space. Although throughout the book are whole group, small group and partner tasks, the improvisations in chapter 5 give special emphasis on the possibilities that partner work can bring. The chapter provides an introduction to contact improvisation and contact work that can lead to further exploration. Chapter 6 of the book investigates how all the wonderful new phrases and sequences created in the previous chapters can be manipulated and developed to help work towards producing a finished piece of choreography.

The improvisations in this book have been tried, tested and adapted to give you the best experience possible. This book is dedicated to all my students who have entered into the spirit of creativity with me at the helm. Enjoy learning and growing with your students, too. And above all, have fun!

Acknowledgements

Thanks to the following:

West Sussex Youth Dance Company, UK
Puppik Dance Company, UK
University College, Chichester, UK
Cathy Childs
Sarah Kate Gardiner
Clive Reeve
Frida Augusta Reeve
Mr. and Mrs. Reeves
The Showroom Theatre, UK
Solent University, Southampton, UK
Caitlin E.G. Reeve

INTRODUCTION TO IMPROVISATION

This chapter describes how to use this book to make the most out of the creative dance experience. It provides tips for planning and running an improvisation session, health and safety considerations and strategies for assessing students.

Preparing to Deliver Dance Improvisation

This book includes step-by-step instructions to guide you through each dance improvisation. Although the improvisations in this book require no previous dance experience, a basic knowledge of dance is invaluable. Regular attendance at dance classes and workshops is helpful for anyone practicing dance improvisation.

A spirit of spontaneous creativity is essential to dance improvisation. Improvisation is like a quick conversation that demands immediate responses, or movement answers. To stay creative within that demand, dancers need to know that no movement answer is wrong. During the improvisation process, encourage dancers to freely explore their movement potential to create innovative dance pieces. Save aesthetic choices for a time later in the creative process, such as when you select the movements that worked well and refine the phrasing.

If you are new to teaching dance, keep in mind that you too can benefit from creative exploration. As you gain more experience you will get a feel for what types of tasks work best for each group of students. It is a good idea to record observations of your present experiences to help you make decisions about how to lead future ones. Encourage your dancers to learn from observation experience, too. Give them opportunities to perform their improvisations for each other and encourage them to observe recordings of their own individual and group performances of improvisations, structured improvisations and developed work. Seeing their work from another perspective is a great way to evaluate their skills and set personal goals.

Leading a dance improvisation requires effective communication with your dancers. During the movement exploration, speak clearly and loudly enough for the group to hear your commands. Between explorations or for complicated instructions, it is helpful to have the group stop moving and sit on the floor so that all dancers can focus and clearly understand your expectations. When talking to your dancers, remember to use positive language to foster the spirit of creative exploration.

All the improvisations in this book can work with small and large groups. Nevertheless, group size does affect the experience. For example, contact improvisation is more challenging and can become unsafe with a larger group. You may decide to use smaller groups for this type of exploration. If you slow the pace with a large group, you can safely make it part of the exploration to observe how group size affects the experience. If you have the luxury of setting your own group sizes, keep them between 10 and 20 dancers for optimal variety while still staying manageable. The size of the space is another factor in deciding group size. Be sure your dancers have enough room to move freely and safely.

The improvisations in this book do not include time limits. How long you spend on each exploration is a personal decision. Individual skill levels, relationships between dancers, ability to focus and other factors affect the duration. Sometimes groups produce interesting results when they have ample time to fully explore movements, and other times they run out of interesting ideas. Experience will teach you and your dancers what is the optimal time to spend on each exploration.

The tasks often refer to terms such as motifs, phrases or sequences. To help you remember these terms, the following list provides analogous terms in literature:

Motif	Chapter title
Phrase	Sentence
Sequence	Paragraph
Section	Chapter
Whole dance composition	Whole book

Planning the Session

The first step in planning your session is to choose a theme to give the class a clear focus. Then, choose improvisations. You can choose any of the improvisations in the book, in any combination. When planning your session, keep in mind the following:

- Choose warm-ups that complement the theme you plan to explore. For example, if you plan to focus on duets, include pair work in the warm-up.
- Choose improvisations that you are comfortable with. If you are uncomfortable, it is not realistic to expect your dancers to be relaxed and open to exploration.
- Carefully assess how many improvisations you need for each session. Too many tasks can cause the dancers and their movements to lose focus.
- Allow ample time for dancers to fully explore their movement potential and enjoy the experience.
- Allow time for evaluation or discussion at the end of the session.
- Be open to changing your plans. Depending on how the dancers are working, you may decide to repeat an improvisation, explore a topic further or add another improvisation.

If you are new to teaching improvisation, it is helpful to start with an existing plan and adapt it as you gain experience. The following workshop plans list improvisations that make up five balanced lessons. These five classes follow a logical course progression and give students a solid foundation for developing improvisation skills. Adapt the plans as necessary to make them effective for your group.

Workshop 1—Topic: Introductions
- Sign In (chapter 3, page 70)
- Greeting and Parting (chapter 3, page 36)
- Introduce the Space (chapter 3, page 56)

Workshop 2—Topic: Restrictions
- Hospital Tag (chapter 2, page 31)
- Restrictions (chapter 4, page 102)

Workshop 3—Topic: Space
- Just Plain Running (chapter 3, page 64)
- Keep the Shape (chapter 3, page 72)
- Encounters (chapter 4, page 116)

Workshop 4—Topic: Duet
- Four in One (chapter 2, page 17)
- Mirror or Follow (chapter 3, page 60)
- Body Part Conversation (chapter 4, page 106)
- Lava Lamp (chapter 5, page 122)

Workshop 5—Topic: Contact

- ✿ Get Knotted (chapter 2, page 21)
- ✿ Energy Impulses (chapter 4, page 78)
- ✿ Clay Sculpting (chapter 5, page 124)
- ✿ Crowd Surfing (chapter 5, page 139)

Sometimes even experienced teachers find themselves at a loss for new ideas. If you need a break from your usual routine but don't know where to turn for inspiration, it is helpful to flip through a list of ideas to find what you are looking for. If you are in that situation, try looking through the Improvisation Finder on page iv. Alternatively, try the improvisations in the following lists. The improvisations here are great staples to keep in your repertoire because you can turn to them for all sorts of sessions.

These improvisations work well with new groups:

- ✿ Greeting and Parting (chapter 3, page 36)
- ✿ Five Seconds (chapter 3, page 38)
- ✿ Circle Dircle (chapter 3, page 52)
- ✿ How Many Body Parts? (chapter 3, page 54)
- ✿ Introduce the Space (chapter 3, page 56)
- ✿ Sign In (chapter 3, page 70)

These improvisations are good for peers to get to know each other:

- ✿ Get Knotted (chapter 2, page 21)
- ✿ Follow You, Follow Me (chapter 2, page 23)
- ✿ This Is Me (chapter 2, page 25)
- ✿ Greeting and Parting (chapter 3, page 36)
- ✿ How Many Body Parts? (chapter 3, page 54)
- ✿ Introduce the Space (chapter 3, page 56)
- ✿ Pass the Movement (chapter 3, page 58)
- ✿ Statues and Speed (chapter 3, page 62)

These improvisations work well to warm up dancers:

- ✿ Cat and Mouse (chapter 2, page 15)
- ✿ Four in One (chapter 2, page 17)
- ✿ Cup of Tea (chapter 2, page 19)
- ✿ Follow You, Follow Me (chapter 2, page 23)
- ✿ Greeting and Parting (chapter 3, page 36)

- Swings and Suspension (chapter 3, page 40)
- Oiling the Joints (chapter 3, page 42)
- Five Curves (chapter 3, page 50)
- How Many Body Parts? (chapter 3, page 54)
- Introduce the Space (chapter 3, page 56)
- Just Plain Running (chapter 3, page 64)
- Touch the Floor (chapter 3, page 66)

Running the Session

Most improvisation sessions follow this order: warm-up, introduction and safety reminders, creation and sharing and discussion and assessment. You may add or omit steps to suit the needs of your class or workshop.

Begin each session with a warm-up to prepare the dancers' bodies and minds for the choreographic tasks ahead. You may use a warm-up task or game from chapter 2 or begin with a technique class. Another choice is to combine them: introduce a warm-up game at the end of technique class.

Once your dancers are warmed up, it is time for them to create and share their movement experiences. Introduce the topic to be explored and discuss safety considerations with the dancers. Each dancer and group is unique and can respond to improvisations differently from day to day. As you get to know your group you can better gauge their abilities and therefore can choose appropriate tasks for them. Dancers work well when each task is time bound so that they have clear deadlines, which could be seconds or minutes. Some groups may work quickly and creatively and may need more input to keep them on task as you wait for all groups to complete the task. Once dancers have shared their work, conclude the session with a discussion.

If one of the tasks doesn't get the response that you want from the dancers, you can always try it again another time with more guidance. You can try another one or even give this book to the dancers to work out the improvisation. You can also repeat the same improvisations or use them again as warm-ups to encourage dancers to develop newer, possibly more mature responses. There is a teaching tip at the end of each improvisation that may assist you in your delivery.

If the dancers have shown clear innovation in their responses or the improvisation has produced original thought, you may want to build on these ideas. Therefore each improvisation includes ideas for longer or future sessions under the Further Development sections.

The improvisations in this book have been created with little or no need for props and other stimuli. However, you can make adaptations to incorporate them into the session. You may even create your own improvisations based on props such as hats, umbrellas, coats, skirts, dresses, suitcases, maps or newspapers. You can use visual stimuli such as photographs, video, paintings, people or places as a starting point when the dancers can think of choreographic tasks to set themselves or their peers. Encourage your dancers to try new and different approaches, ideas and ways of working.

Health and Safety Considerations

Before you begin a task, it is worthwhile to discuss health and safety with your dancers. In addition to creative skills, dancers need to develop safety awareness, muscular strength and a sense of responsibility for the health and safety of the group. For example, injuries such as falls can occur during lifts and counterbalances. Knowledge of weight transfer principles, proper lifting technique and each dancer's physical strengths and weaknesses can help prevent such injuries. Consider incorporating strength exercises into the warm-up and clearly discuss safety tips and expectations before embarking on a movement investigation.

Before each session, be sure to prepare the space and discuss safety concerns with your dancers. The following are tips for both the teacher and the dancers:

Environmental Considerations for the Teacher

- **Floors.** Are they sprung? If you are moving on a hard floor, jumping and travelling will cause injuries such as shinsplints and stress fractures.
- **Hot temperature.** Is the room or space too hot? The body needs fluid to help its own cooling system (sweating) and a dancer may become dehydrated or have muscle spasms resulting from depletion of body salts.
- **Cold temperature.** This is dangerous because muscles find it hard to work properly and can be easily torn. If this cannot be helped movers need to wear warm clothes and be aware as they take off the layers that muscles need to remain warm and that opening a window with a rush of cold air can also cause muscles to tear.
- **Hazards.** Make sure the space is free of obstacles and check the floor for sharp objects.

Health and Safety Tips for Dancers

- Be aware of your own strengths and weaknesses and do not attempt something that will cause injury.
- Always concentrate with great intensity. If you lose concentration, stop the activity.
- Recognise warning signs of fatigue, which may include dizziness or shaking muscles. An injury can happen when a dancer does not attempt a movement correctly and tries to cut corners. It may be necessary to cut back on either the intensity or the activity that causes fatigue.
- Practice good health habits to keep you strong and focused, such as balanced eating, proper hydration, adequate sleep and avoiding drugs.
- Always do a proper warm-up.
- Be aware of the number of dancers in the room to avoid any collisions that can happen with large groups or if you are closing your eyes.
- Follow proper lifting techniques. In some cases it may be as simple as bending the knees and not lifting with the back. It makes sense for the lifter not to lift a load that is too heavy. The lifted dancer also needs the correct support so that they don't fall; this includes having other people available and aware of the actions to guide the lift. For the dancer being lifted, they need to give their weight appropriately and be aware at all times of how they could come out of the lift at every stage.
- Hygiene is an important health consideration, especially when working in groups.
- When a dancer comes to class sick or becomes sick during the workshop, it is a concern for the health of the group. You may have your own systems in place but it is good practice to try and avoid having these dancers in class. They should take the initiative and remove themselves from class.
- Follow the correct dress code for dance. This includes removing jewelry, watches and any other items of clothing that could harm a partner.

Discussion and Assessment Strategies

As you try the improvisations in this book, you will observe diverse movement answers from every dancer. You and your students will see actions and phrases that you like and ones that you dislike, and your opinions will vary as much as your knowledge and experiences vary. The ability to discuss these opinions is an important skill in the improvisation process, so encourage all your dancers to participate in discussions. As dancers begin to discuss their observations, they experience dance from another perspective and they increase their ability to express ideas verbally. Listening to the discussion can give you a clearer idea of what the dancers understand about their creations. Some improvisations in this book include cues for encouraging discussion. Use your own ideas for questions and discussion sessions, too.

A good way to encourage discussion is to consistently include a discussion session after groups share their work. Ask students to make positive, constructive comments using terms such as *relationships, actions, dynamics and space (RADS)*. Remind them that all interpretations are valid, so they can discuss how something made them feel or what they liked about it. Rather than discuss *dis*likes, ask students what they would do to turn the improvisation into a theatre performance.

For the purpose of class discussion, analysis or data collection, the best way to capture the creations made through improvisation is by video, but you may not want to use it in every session. Sometimes a video camera can change the dancers' focus; they may either play to the camera or be shy about trying new things. You may find that asking the dancers to write a few notes or ideas in a choreographic logbook or diary will feed their future creations.

If dancers create something that you would like to keep and use, another way to capture the creation is to teach it to the entire class so that someone will remember it in the next session. This may be difficult if you are teaching infrequently or have a two-week timetable. Consider using a video camera at the end of a session.

Some courses in the United Kingdom emphasise collecting evidence of skills acquired against grading criteria or mark schemes. Even if not required, analysing data and processes can aid learning and assessment. You may collect evidence for assessment as a tutor observation and feedback, which could be in the form of notes, memory or a devised form. It could be dancer evaluations, peer feedback and witness statement or even audience feedback. The simplest and quickest way to collect evidence is to use a form on which the tutor can check boxes. You could also give the form to the dancers to assess themselves or to assess a peer.

Dancers who achieve highly in these tasks will have an elegance about their work and a greater understanding of the movement choices they are making in response to other dancers.

Following is a form that you and your dancers may find helpful. One page is directed toward the teacher and the other is directed toward the dancer, but either party can use either page at any point. The first page is a simple sheet containing boxes to check that gives your students a chance to see your impression of how they are doing in workshops. It also provides the vocabulary that they can then use for themselves in the second sheet. Dancers can use this tick box sheet for a quick self-assessment or peer assessment. The second page demands that the dancers start to now use these dance terms in describing their own strengths and weaknesses—something that is now at the heart of most curricula, whether they be physical education or dance. Once a dancer has addressed their own strengths and weaknesses, they can use this to set goals or targets for themselves for future workshops. These goals can then be reviewed over time and perhaps achieved and replaced with more challenging goals by the dancer or the tutor. The sheet will prompt the dancers to think about how they are doing and give them some simple terminology to describe what they may want to achieve.

Assessment Toolbox

Date _____

Page 1: Teacher

Working well in workshops	Needs improvement	Satisfactory	Good	Very good	Excellent
Attendance					
Working co-operatively					
Level of commitment					
Level of discipline					

Improvisation skills	Needs improvement	Satisfactory	Good	Very good	Excellent
Ability to apply improvisation methods					
Responding in a considered way					
Using insight in improvisations					
A willingness to go beyond exploring the obvious					
Communicating the themes of the improvisation					
Ability to reproduce movement accurately					
Using technical ability					
Relationships to other dancers					
Spatial awareness					

Performance skills	Needs improvement	Satisfactory	Good	Very good	Excellent
Musicality (when relevant)					
Focus					
Emphasis					
Facial expression					
Dynamic range					

From J. Reeve, 2011, *Dance improvisations* (Champaign, IL: Human Kinetics).

10

Assessment Toolbox

Page 2: Dancer

STRENGTHS		
Working well in workshops	**Improvisation skills**	**Performance skills**

WEAKNESSES		
Working well in workshops	**Improvisation skills**	**Performance skills**

Targets (personal goals that a dancer or tutor can set once the above information has been completed)	Needs improvement	Satisfactory	Good	Very good	Excellent

From J. Reeve, 2011, *Dance improvisations* (Champaign, IL: Human Kinetics).

CHAPTER 2

WARM-UP IMPROVISATIONS

se the improvisations in this chapter to prepare your students physically and mentally for the creative tasks ahead. These warm-ups get dancers working productively in the space, raise their heart rates and prepare them to focus on the rest of the workshop. You can use the warm-up improvisations in developing choreography, too. The Further Development section at the end of each improvisation provides suggestions for taking it to the next level.

Warming up is vital for your dancers' safety and therefore it must be included in every session. Advantages of warming up include the following:

1. It increases the heart rate, which increases blood flow to the muscles, supplying them with the oxygen they need in order to work efficiently.

2. Increasing blood flow aids in the removal of muscle waste such as lactic acid and is believed to relieve the feeling of soreness.

3. It increases body temperature, which allows for safer stretching of muscles.

4. It increases the depth and rate of breathing required to achieve the appropriate level for the ensuing exercise.

5. It increases the supply of synovial fluid to the joints. This fluid lubricates the joints and increases their range of motion, whilst decreasing their injury potential.

6. It improves circulation to dilate (open up) the skin vessels in order to allow body temperature to be maintained at safe levels.

You can decide to do just one warm-up improvisation and then move on to the main topic of the class, or you can do several warm-ups. The important consideration is that all dancers are warm, have increased their heart rates and are mentally ready for the next task. The first improvisation, Cat and Mouse, works well as a single warm-up. It gets all the dancers moving at some point and it can continue for up to 20 minutes. Some groups may benefit from several consecutive warm-up improvisations to train their response time. For example, you could use Sign In to get them all together facing the centre, ready to begin. Next you could use Four in One to prompt individual quick creative responses and Mirror or Follow to get them effectively working in pairs. Be careful not to overwhelm dancers with too many warm-ups, though. They need to be focused and not fatigued before the next task.

Cat and Mouse

This game warms up the body and is beneficial for new groups in a new space. Students will be running and dodging, so please ensure that the floor and footwear are not slippery. Bare feet are ideal for this game.

Everyone is involved as one dancer chases another.

1. Choose one person to be the cat and another to be the mouse. These roles will change constantly throughout the game.

2. Ask the remaining students to link arms with one or two other people; everyone is in a group of either two or three people linked together.

3. Have the groups spread out in the dance space to create stationary safe houses for the mouse.

4. The game begins when the cat chases the mouse. If the cat tags the mouse, they swap roles; the cat becomes the mouse and the mouse becomes the cat.

5. If the mouse links arms with one of the dancers who form the safe houses, the dancer at the end of the line becomes the mouse and must let go.

6. In this arrangement, chances are high that every student can have a chance to be the mouse. They can become the cat only if caught by the cat.

7. This is a fast-paced game in which roles change quickly. Dancers need to observe the cat and mouse even if they are standing still; at any time they could become the mouse and have to run.

Teaching Tip

Have dancers try various ways to travel, such as galloping, skipping, rolling or jumping. They could also use known travelling sequences.

Further Development

You can use this notion of one dancer releasing another to move within a piece of choreography. For example, have dancers create group tableaux (moments of stillness) and then nudge, link, grab or push other dancers to move. You can use this idea with Statues and Speed (page 62).

Four in One

This series of quick improvisational games encourages new groups to work together in a fun way. It works well at the beginning of a term. It also introduces dancers to partner work.

1. You may want to include a warm-up game before this game to get the focus of the group.

2. **Game 1: sword fight.** Have dancers find a partner and then find a space in the room away from other dancers, facing each other. Both dancers place one hand, palm open, on their own lower back; this is a target. The index finger of the other hand is pointed towards the partner; this is a sword. On the command "Go," the dancers use the sword to make contact with the opponent's target. They may stay on the spot or travel around the room; each couple will find their own way of playing. You can make rules for winning the game, such as the first one to score three touches is the winner or the first one to make contact is the winner. You can have dancers swap partners and have another match. You can have a tournament in which winners play winners until one person ultimately wins.

3. **Game 2: take off the crown.** Next, to keep the energy going, the dancers must find a new partner to form a new duo and a new space in the room. Partner A places one hand on the top of the head; the palm makes contact with the crown. On the command "Go," partner B tries to break the head–hand connection. The dancers will find their own way of playing; perhaps they will drag their partners around the room or tickle them. As a rule, this action is usually impossible and is meant to be so in this game. As in game 1, dancers can swap partners and have another match in which winners play winners.

Partner B's attempt to take Partner A's hand off her crown.

4. **Game 3: turtle turning.** Have dancers begin with new partners again; they should work with a completely new person each time. In this game, one partner, the turtle, lies prone on the floor and makes a star shape with the limbs straight. On the command "Go," the standing partner must try to turn the turtle over. When they have either succeeded or failed, ask dancers to swap places and play again. This task is also meant to be impossible.

One dancer experiments with turning over the "turtle."

5. **Game 4: hands on knees.** Have dancers choose new partners and face each other with their hands on their own knees. The object of the game is to touch the opponent's knees with both hands. If their hands are on their knees and they touch hands instead of knees, they cannot score. This action could lead to stalemate or the dancers could tease each other by exposing their knees.

Teaching Tip

Have the dancers control and vary their speed; they can slow down or move faster. It is helpful to use two contrasting pieces of music or a piece with varying tempos.

Further Development

This could lead into The Connection (page 120).

Cup of Tea

This warm-up game raises the heart rate to improve stamina. It can benefit new groups working in a new space. Dancers will be running and dodging, so ensure that the floor and footwear or bare feet are not slippery.

Several cups of tea capturing dancers.

1. Choose one dancer to be the first cup of tea and who tries to capture a partner. The captured partner then becomes a cup of tea.

2. Have the remaining students split into two groups and separate to the two opposite sides of the room, which will be their safe houses.

3. The cup of tea uses the arms to make the shape of a circle in front of the body (first position) and joins the hands together. To capture a partner the circle passes over the partner's head. The captured dancer then becomes a cup of tea.

4. As the other dancers leave their safe house to cross the room to the other side, which is also a safe house, they must say, "Cup of tea" as fast and as many times as they can with only one breath. If they inhale before reaching the other safe house, they must stop and

become a still cup of tea where they ran out of breath. So, they will create the circular arm position once they are still and then begin to try to catch other dancers also in this shape.

5. The growing number of moving cups of tea, including the original one, will remain cups of tea until everyone has been captured. Then a new game may start with a different person starting as the one cup of tea.

Teaching Tip

Try having the first captured dancer join the first cup of tea person and help them to capture other members of the group. This choice will result in a faster improvisation in which most dancers try to capture a few.

Further Development

Extend the concept of completing an action using only one breath to other improvisations. Think of other warm-ups in which dancers make a decision before the breath runs out.

Get Knotted

This improvisation works well with new groups. You can use it to introduce dancers to each other, as a problem to solve, as a warm-up for a contact session or as a team-building exercise.

1. Ask the group to form a large circle. To ensure that dancers are evenly spaced, ask them to be the same distance from the dancer on their right as from the dancer on their left. Then ask them to face the centre of the circle and hold hands.

2. Keeping their hands held, the dancers attempt to make a knot by stepping over or going under the arms of two others.

3. To untie the knot, dancers can either let go of their hands or retrace their actions, which gives them the chance to retrograde.

4. Next, the dancers make a circle that is much tighter so that they are almost shoulder to shoulder. Then they close their eyes, extend both arms forward into the middle of the circle and grab the hands of two other dancers that are not next to them. They can reach across the circle or even cross the arms. They usually end up holding the hands of two different dancers.

The group reaches to find hands to hold with the eyes closed.

5. Have the dancers open their eyes to see where they are and, as a whole group, try to unravel themselves. They can talk to each other at first if they need to be guided but it is ideal to complete this task in silence. To add an element of competition you could time the task. You can see if at a later date they can break their record time or you can allocate a specific amount of time for them to succeed.

6. Have dancers repeat the reaching and finding of other arms to grab, but without talking and as quickly as possible. Sometimes, especially with a large group, when all are unravelled there may be more than one circle of dancers.

7. Next, split the group in half and try again with two smaller groups. This time it could be competitive to see which group can unravel first. If the groups cheat and just hold the hands of the dancers next to them before unravelling, ask one dancer to physically make the connections of one hand to another.

Teaching Tip

Try changing the size of your group. If you start with a large group, you can change to multiple smaller groups. If dancers remember what movements they did to unravel, they could try repeating the experience to music and even try to make the group travel as they unravel. You could also put a dancer in the middle of the circle and they could unravel the bodies without talking.

The group unravels with the eyes open.

Further Development

This task could lead into contact work where dancers are lifted over arms. If two circles are linked the dancers could lift each other or have their weight supported as they roll over and climb through the group. This could be the main theme in a trio incorporating rond de jambe movements, counterbalances, supports, turns or jumps, whilst the dancers hold hands and create new shapes.

Follow You, Follow Me

This warm-up raises the heart rate while helping new students get used to a new space. It is also a good way to introduce dancers to improvising where they have to pre-empt, react, and respond in the moment. Students will be travelling and changing direction, so ensure that the floor and footwear or bare feet are not slippery.

The group plays follow the leader.

1. Start the session with a game of follow the leader, in which one dancer moves around the space and all the other dancers follow and copy their actions. If you have a confident group you can let them decide when to be in the leader role by saying, "Let's all be me." This will prompt all the other dancers to copy and follow them. This can happen as many times as you like or until all dancers have led the class. Alternatively, you can call out the names of dancers to be leaders and give it a time limit from 10 seconds to 10 minutes, depending on what works best for your group.

2. At first the dancers may struggle with the selection of movement material. They can limit their movements by copying actions that the previous leader performed. Nevertheless, most groups will run around the room and after 25 people have led the group they

are tired. To keep this warm-up interesting but not exhausting, you can have dancers do it several times over a period of time, each time with a different dancer leading. For example, you could go through only five leaders for each warm-up session until all the dancers have been the leader. It also helps to set a standard for what types of movements you expect them to perform so that the leader helps to warm up the group appropriately.

3. As each dancer leads, try calling out a body action that needs to appear in the movements. For example, "Jump, turn and fall." If movements are limited and dancers are still self-conscious the first time they do this task, count 5 to 10 seconds before handing over leadership to another dancer.

4. Have dancers play follow the leader in smaller groups of four or five. Groups may have to pass through, go around, go over or go under other groups. You can create the obstacles by getting half of the groups to freeze at a given point while the other groups continue to move in the space. To continue changing leaders in multiple groups, try having the dancers number themselves within each group, then call out a number to indicate who is the leader. For example, for groups of five, dancers are numbered 1, 2, 3, 4 and 5.

5. Stop the group when the smaller group task has worked successfully, and set up the next stage by asking them to try to follow the leader of the group without discussing anything during the task itself. This will mean that they will have to frequently swap over the role of being the leader and to have all been the leader in the time given. The dancers may find it a challenge to take the lead without discussion but it will start to develop their unspoken dance language.

Teaching Tip

You can incorporate learning the main body actions in this task. For example, ask each group to focus on three body actions at a time. One group could play with gesture, turning and travelling; another could play with falling, travelling and stillness; and another could play with balance, jumping and gesture.

Further Development

Once the dancers have developed a sense of what other members of a group are doing, have them try the contact improvisation exercises found in chapter 5 that demand this type of awareness.

This Is Me

This improvisation can help you get to know the names of new students and gives them a chance to interact with each other. To build confidence needed for this improvisation, you may want to do Five Seconds (page 38) first.

1. Ask the dancers to form a large circle in the space. To ensure that dancers are evenly spaced, ask them to be the same distance from the dancer on their right as from the dancer on their left. The circle needs to be as big as possible so that the space in the middle is big enough to dance in.

2. Ask the dancers to enter the circle one by one, then say their name clearly and perform any movement that they like. It could be something that they love to do such as a gesture or jump. It should be something that they think of as unique to them. Try not to give them too much time to think about it. If they are struggling you could ask them to just stand in the circle and say their name; they most likely will do a movement, such as a gesture, without even thinking. If you have a shy group of dancers who don't seem to want to go into the circle, they could do the action where they are standing.

3. After a dancer speaks and moves, all the dancers then repeat that dancer's name out loud and perform the movement all together.

To get to know each other, dancers enter the circle one by one and perform any movement they like.

If dancers are new and feel self-conscious, they can still participate by repeating the names and movements of other dancers until they are ready for their turn.

4. Once all dancers have had a turn speaking and moving, ask all the dancers to quickly perform all the actions with names that they can remember.

5. Next, ask the dancers to walk around the room and to approach other dancers and see if they can perform their own actions back to them. If they can't remember, they can ask to see them again. See if they can show everyone their actions.

6. Next, ask the dancers to add another movement to their original introduction and perform it without saying their name. They can do this back in a circle.

7. Ask the dancers to enter the circle two or three at a time and see how their movements and shapes can be complimented or counterbalanced with the other dancers. How could they fit together? Back to back? Facing each other? Side by side? Ask the dancers watching what works and have them give directions.

8. Try putting the dancers into small groups of three or four. Ask every dancer to learn the movements of the whole group, then put them together to make a longer phrase.

9. From this phrase you could ask the groups to add in anything: a jump, make one movement travel, change the timing or repeat a movement. For some contrast you could ask that they try a canon movement, two dancers jump whilst the other two go into the floor or to change the staging of the group twice.

10. Before they show the rest of the groups ask them to find a way of coming into the performance space and a way of leaving, deciding where they want to enter from and exit to.

Teaching Tip

Walking around and greeting each other may be difficult in a larger group because dancers may stop to chat, so stay involved by walking around, too. If it doesn't work this way, ask the dancers to greet each other in the middle of the circle, making sure the circle is never empty and that all dancers have gone in three times each.

Further Development

Take two dancers from one of the smaller groups and put them into another group. Ask them to learn each other's sequence or phrase and add it together with their own group's phrase. Then, keep combining groups until you have longer quartets that have everyone's introduction movement in them.

Chase the Mouse

This warm-up game is beneficial for new groups in a new space. The students will be running and dodging, so ensure that the floor and footwear or bare feet are not slippery.

1. Choose one person to be the cat and another to be the mouse.

2. The other dancers make rows of equal numbers, such as maybe four rows of five dancers evenly spaced. The dancers must leave enough of a gap for the cat or mouse to run between them.

3. The dancers must decide which way the lines are going to be enforced by linking hands or arms. The lines could be vertical or horizontal: Each dancer could link hands with the dancer next to them or the dancers behind and in front of them.

Dancers hold hands and form horizontal lines.

4. Movement begins when the cat chases the mouse. You can give the signal "Change" for the lines to change direction to block a pathway, they could turn to face front, or turn to face the side.

5. Once the cat has caught the mouse, they reverse roles.

6. Select a new cat and mouse if desired.

Teaching Tip

This is a good way to get groups to form lines and spread out for warm-ups and more technical class work.

Further Development

You can introduce a different quality to a sequence by using the notion of stopping a dancer from moving into a new place. Doing so can further define the dance space. You can have dancers tag other dancers in a given formation in the space to make a sequence travel. You can make the movement content more spontaneous by shouting out a movement; in fact, anyone could shout from a range of signals to create a structured improvisation.

Focus Up

This is a quick improvisation that is good for getting the group to focus. It is especially useful before dancers perform on stage. It helps dancers think about the connections that they have with the other dancers in the group.

1. Ask the dancers to form a circle in the space. To ensure that dancers are evenly spaced, ask them to be the same distance from the dancer on their right as from the dancer on their left. The circle can be any size to fit the space; you can even make a small circle in a dressing room, but dancers must be standing.

2. This task has two simple actions: on the command "Focus down," look at the floor; on the command "Focus up," look another dancer in the eye.

3. Say, "Focus down." The dancers should look at the floor. At this point they need to think and maybe even feel who they want to look at when they look up.

4. Say, "Focus up." The dancers should look only one other dancer in the eye; once they are looking at someone, they may not choose another dancer. If two dancers are looking directly at each other, they can sit down.

Dancers respond to the command, "Focus up."

5. The commands start again until everyone is sitting down. If the dancers are connecting well with each other, it is possible to have everyone sitting down after saying "Focus up" just three times.

Teaching Tip

You can start in a small circle, then make the circle bigger and eventually get the dancers walking around the space as they look up and down.

Further Development

You can add new commands. For example, say, "Point out" to get dancers to point a finger at the same time as they focus eyes on another dancer. Another option is to get dancers to sit or to stand on one leg. You can also add new consequences. For example, instead of having dancers sit down, you might have them meet at the centre of the circle and hold hands. This consequence can lead to a contact improvisation.

Hospital Tag

This game warms up the body and is beneficial to new groups in a new space. Students will be running and dodging, so ensure that the floor and footwear or bare feet are not slippery.

Each time a dancer is tagged, a new restriction is imposed such as having to put one arm behind the back.

1. As in playground tag, one dancer takes the role of It. The dancer runs around the space trying to tag as many other dancers as possible in a given time.

2. The other dancers must try to get away but can be tagged four times until they are out.

    a. The first time a dancer is tagged, one arm goes behind the back.

    b. The second time a dancer is tagged, both arms go behind the back.

    c. The third time a dancer is tagged, both arms stay behind the back while the dancer hops on one leg.

    d. The fourth time the dancer is tagged, the dancer must roll on the floor without using the arms, if possible.

3. If a dancer is then tagged whilst on the floor, the dancer must leave the space and go to an area of the room called the hospital. There the dancer must perform a specified movement for a given period of time, such as standing on one leg with the arms flapping like wings for 1 minute.

4. After a given period of time, choose the next It from the dancers in the hospital. As the dancers gradually find it difficult to travel the game will move more quickly, but giving it a short time scale can stop the dancers from losing focus.

5. Although restricted movements are challenging, this warm-up is meant to be fun, so use it with dancers that have a good sense of humour.

Teaching Tip

This game is useful for small groups and you can even use it with pairs. It can work well as a game with a clear winner or as a choreographic task layered onto a known dance sequence; as the dancers are tagged, the sequence changes.

Further Development

This notion of having a restriction whilst moving is explored further in the Further Development section of the RADS and Restrictions (page 151) task.

Who Started That?

This is a quick warm-up improvisation for new and younger groups. It requires them to respond quickly to movements created by another peer but without the central person knowing who started the movement.

1. Ask the dancers to form a circle in the space. To ensure that dancers are evenly spaced, ask them to be the same distance from the dancer on their right as from the dancer on their left.

2. Choose one dancer to play the role of the central guesser. Have the guesser turn around or close the eyes while you choose another dancer as the leader.

3. The leader makes small dance movements that anyone else in the circle can copy at any time. Each time they make a gesture, turn, jump or any other movement it must be different.

One dancer has just discovered who "started that."

4. The central guesser watches the movements in the circle and tries to guess who the leader is. If the guesser is correct, the leader enters the circle and becomes the guesser for the next round of the game.

Teaching Tip

If possible, send the guesser out of the room while you choose the leader. You could also have dancers choose a piece of paper from a hat; the one who chooses the one marked "leader" is the leader.

Further Development

This task gets dancers thinking about synchronising movements and what a canon is. It could lead into a simple structured improvisation in which the dancers choose to follow three different leaders, changing who they follow from moment to moment.

CHAPTER 3

CREATING MOVEMENT MATERIAL

The improvisations in this chapter have a dual purpose. They can prepare your dancers to dance, and they form a good base for creating and developing interesting movement material. *Movement material* refers to actions, motifs, phrases and sequences—moments of dance that may not yet be ordered into choreography, or dance composition. Creating movement material is like designing clothes. A designer cuts the cloth, or material, into different patterns and pieces it together to create a complete composition. A choreographer uses movement material to create a longer sequence of movements, or whole dance composition. It is rare for a contemporary dance choreographer to start creating a dance at the beginning and work through a piece to the end. The common practice is to create all the movement material first and then start the craft of developing and structuring the dance, similar to the way a tailor may make a jacket.

Greeting and Parting

This warm-up task is beneficial for introducing new groups to a new space. The students will be running and dodging, so ensure that the floor and footwear or bare feet are not slippery. It can also get dancers thinking about creating original movements and therefore great to use at the beginning of a new term or semester.

Dancers greet partners and perform their unique gestures.

1. Have dancers find a partner. You can use groups of three if needed.

2. Ask the dancers to face each other and introduce themselves; they can ask for each other's names and one other question to keep on task.

3. Ask the pairs to explore original ways of saying hello to each other and to create a final short phrase with more than one movement. You can inspire original movement by suggesting that they are aliens who have developed their own movement language. Then say, "Hello" as their cue to perform this new greeting.

4. Next, dancers create a phrase for goodbye, which is somehow different from the first phrase. Say, "Goodbye" as their cue to perform the parting. Ask the dancers to try both the phrases to see how long they are; you may suggest that some duos extend phrases that

are too short in relation to the whole group. Once the greetings are established, the dancers can use them each time they meet and part. Ask the pairs to remember exactly where they are in the space; they will return to this place at the end of their space exploration.

5. Have the dancers explore the space in the room for a certain number of counts before they return to where they started and greet their partners. The dancers should travel around the whole room, through every bit of space, at every level so that if you took a slow photograph you could see a trace of where they have been almost everywhere in the space. Try this exploration of space in 16 counts, 8 counts, 4 counts, 2 counts and finally 1 count, which can be quite a challenge. Each time the dancers part to explore the space, they must perform their parting phrase first. You can keep the dancers on task by saying "Goodbye" and "Hello" while counting out loud. End the task with the partners greeting each other in their original part of the space. For a faster pace, try using only 2 counts and then 1 count several times. See what happens to the movements when you quickly say, "Goodbye, count 1, hello" repeatedly.

Teaching Tip

Have each pair show both their hello and goodbye movements to the rest of the group. The dancers can see how different and possibly interesting their fellow dancers' movements are and be inspired to improve their own. The idea of the dancers being in space, greeting each other as aliens and exploring a new planet works well with younger groups.

Further Development

Combine pairs into groups of four and have them learn each other's greeting and parting movements. You can develop this improvisation into a whole group section of a dance piece in which you play with simple unison and canon work.

Five Seconds

This exercise works well to introduce new groups at the beginning of a session, and it helps to develop confidence. It can also be used at any point in the term as it can remind dancers what it feels like to perform a solo with given or longer movement material.

1. Ask the dancers to form a large circle in the space. To ensure that dancers are evenly spaced, ask them to be the same distance from the dancer on their right as from the dancer on their left. You, the teacher, also need to be part of the circle.

2. Ask the dancers to go into the circle one at a time and perform any dance they choose—a tap step, a break dance move, ballet or any choreography. It could even include text, a joke or a song. Each dancer performs for 5 seconds. Count this time out loud so that the dancers don't cut their time in the circle short. Explain to the dancers that the whole group loves dance so much; whenever they see it performed they clap and cheer.

3. As soon as each performance is finished, the rest of the circle must applaud and cheer. You may need to keep the momentum and enthusiasm for cheering going until every dancer has performed so that each dancer gets the same response. If dancers are nervous or can't think of anything to do in the circle, let

A group of dancers applauds one dancer in the centre.

them know that they can hold a position; stillness is still dance. They can walk into the circle, sit down and then leave.

4. After all the dancers have had a go in the circle, ask them a few questions to see how they got on. Ask the dancers to put their hands up if they liked doing that exercise, they didn't enjoy it much, they didn't know what to do, they would have liked more time, they would perform the same thing if they did it again or they would do something different next time. You may want to do it again after you get these responses.

5. Try the exercise again, this time asking dancers to perform certain movements when they are in the circle. For example, ask them to do only jumps and turns. If the whole group is not too tired of this exercise, each dancer could be in the circle for longer periods of time while the others maintain the applause.

6. Try this exercise on another day, this time making the time 7 seconds. More time in the circle can help build confidence.

Teaching Tip

Turn the circle into something more like a stage setting. Ask the audience to form in a given part of the space. Have each performer enter from the side (stage right), walk into the centre, perform one movement and then exit the space (stage left). You can decide if the audience applauds when the dancer exits or if they can keep it going from when they enter until they exit.

Further Development

This task could lead into Sign In (page 70) or any other improvisation in which performing may be an outcome.

Swings and Suspension

One key aspect of contemporary dance is that it uses breath to aid jumps, suspension, swings, falls and sequences with an ongoing feel. Swings function to both warm the body up and train the dancer to use body weight to travel with suspension and breath, which can aid balance and quality. Swings are also useful for creating high points in phrases of choreography.

1. Ask the dancers to experiment with different ways the arms can swing using all three planes. The sagittal, also known as the wheel plane, is a joining of depth and height. The vertical—or the door plane—is a joining of height and width and the horizontal—or the table plane—is a joining of width and depth. For example, in the sagittal (wheel) plane they could try circling the arms forward together in a circle, back to parallel high and reversing this movement, then adding knee bends or even a jump. You may want to have music playing in the background to aid counts and dynamics.

Dancers at different stages of the swing.

2. If dancers need more direction from you, tell them some of these ideas: Have them swing forwards from parallel high, circle the arms but take the body forwards and bring the arms and the body back up; dancers can swing with or without knee bends. Have them circle the arms once with a knee bend, taking the arms and body over with a knee bend. If dancers straighten the knees when they are upside down, circle the arms backwards whilst bringing the body up and then complete another circle with a knee bend, they can create a short phrase. Using one arm and then the other arm could help develop this movement. As the dancers explore the notion of swing with the arms, ask them, "How could you incorporate the torso in these movements? When could the actions drop forward with the torso?"

3. Have the dancers face each other in pairs and decide who will perform their improvisation first whilst the other one mirrors. Ask them to think about where the suspension is and see if they can inhale at the right points. The dancers also need to swap roles. You could also ask the dancers to develop their arm swings using different ways of travelling, exploring where the whole body could go in the space.

4. Next, ask the dancers to explore moving using the other two planes. Here are some ideas for exploration: Have them spread out in the space so that they don't collide. They can swing the arms horizontally around the torso, wrapping them around the body. They can change the size of the arm movement and add levels and even jumps with changes of facing. They can reach the arms up to the top diagonal, let them swing down and up to the opposite side, even completing a circle back to where they started and maybe add a gallop.

5. Ask the pairs to create a swing phrase that uses suspension and breath. Ask them to watch each other and give feedback to see if they are in at the top of the swing and that there is a change in dynamic as gravity takes over. Ask dancers to perform their phrases for the rest of the class.

Teaching Tip

The dancers may want to work in pairs from the beginning and not come together only to share.

Further Development

Dancers can use the phrases they created in any choreography or as warm-ups for future workshops. You may want to record the dancers on video in case they or you forget the sequences.

Oiling the Joints

You can use this task at the beginning of a creative session or technique class. When warming up the body, try to identify the bones and the joints used to make the dancers aware of what is moving and how it is moving. This improvisation gives a general insight into release technique.

1. Ask the dancers to find a space away from other dancers and choose a facing. You can get students to face the front, but this may give the improvisation too much of a technique feel. Ask the dancers to close the eyes and focus the mind first on sounds that they can hear in the room, then sounds outside the room and finally the noises inside the body. Not all dancers will close the eyes, but remember to ask them to open the eyes at the end.

2. Dancers stand in a parallel or relaxed stance. Ask them to shift the body weight forwards, then backwards whilst maintaining their posture and to sway side to side with the feet fixed to the floor. They can keep the eyes open or closed.

3. Have dancers increase this play with their balance; for example, they can fall forwards whilst keeping the connection to the floor with the feet. They could also take the body weight to the side until the point at which they have to stop themselves somehow from falling.

4. Next, talk them through their stance. For example,

Letting gravity move the body can lead dancers to move the exercise to the floor.

"Soften your knees, releasing any tension, and allow the patella to have the feeling of falling towards the floor." This may encourage the dancers to slightly bend their knees but be aware of how they are holding tension in the body. You could also ask them "to be aware of your spine from your head (skull) to your coccyx (tailbone) in all movements." Encouraging the dancers to consider their inner space will connect them with how dance feels.

5. Explore each joint's range of movement: flexing, extending and rotating. Ask the dancers where the body weight is and at what point can they balance or stop with little effort.

6. This notion of letting gravity move the body can lead the exercise to the floor. Have the dancers lie supine and raise one leg straight up, finding where the leg can go so that it almost balances with little effort. Using gravity to flex at the knee, dancers place the foot on the floor and then let the foot slide along the floor until the leg is straight. The dancers can repeat this exercise several times with each leg. It feels as if the leg is drawing a circle using its own weight to move.

7. While dancers are still lying down, ask them to bend both knees and place the feet on the floor. Then, instruct them to let both knees drop to one side and then the other to feel a stretch in the lower back.

8. These movements may lead into rolling along the floor; a leg or an arm can initiate the motion.

Teaching Tip

Discuss how gravity can aid these movements, where the movements initiate in the body and where their weight wants to take them. Dancers may want to investigate release technique ideas for performance pieces.

Further Development

This task is ideal for focusing a group before exams and performances or just a great way to get a group to be quiet and considerate, leaving the day outside the dance studio.

Signals and Pulses

This improvisation encourages dancers to explore what happens inside the body during movement. This heightened body awareness can help improve overall performance skills. When warming up the dancers before this improvisation, try to identify the impulse of energy, where it starts in the body and where it can travel.

1. Ask the dancers to find a space away from other dancers and choose a facing. You can get students to face the front, but this may give the improvisation a technique feel. Ask the dancers to focus their minds on the sounds of their own breathing.

2. Have dancers standing in a parallel or relaxed stance. Ask them to pick a part of the body to move and explore different ways of moving that part (Does it flex, extend or rotate? Can it do all of these movements at once?) Dancers need to identify where the energy comes from to perform that particular movement. They may be able to feel which muscles help to initiate the movement.

Dancers discover how a body part can move.

3. Ask the dancers to pick a second body part and explore how movements are initiated. Observe the dancers' movement answers. If their exploration is limited, you can encourage further exploration by adding different qualities to the movement. For example, you can say, "How slow, small, big, jerky, erratic can you move that part?"

4. Ask the dancers to imagine a pathway of energy that travels within the body, between the two parts they have explored. If dancers do not grasp this idea at first, you may do a simple demonstration to get them started.

5. Then, ask dancers to allow impulses of movement to flow seamlessly along different pathways through the body. The goal is to create natural, fluid movements.

6. Once dancers have explored their own movements, have them show a partner; they can guess where the movement was initiated in the body and where it finished.

7. Ask dancers to create a movement phrase in which movement is initiated in one body part and travels through five more body parts before the energy is released from the body. Your students' movement answers will vary.

Teaching Tip

Music affects the overall feel of this improvisation. If you choose to use music, the style you choose can help vary the speeds and qualities of the dancers' movements, raising their level of sophistication.

Further Development

In order to allow the dancers to watch and discuss what they have performed, set up performance pairs. Ask dancers to show their phrases to their partners, beginning and ending with a moment of stillness. The partners then list the body parts that they saw the movements pass through. If they missed a body part, the choreographer figures out how to make it stand out more clearly. You can have dancers dance their partners' phrases back to them. This is a great way to see what stands out in choreography. Ask, "What did your partner remember?"

Signal Circle

This improvisation is a good warm-up for dancers who have trouble with Signals and Pulses (page 44). It uses the principles of signals and pulses as they move outside the body and pass to other dancers across the space. Doing some isolations can help prepare the body for this improvisation.

1. Ask the dancers to find a space in a circle, making sure that they are the same distance from the person on the left and the person on the right.

2. Have dancers stand in a parallel or relaxed stance. Ask them to imagine a pathway of energy that travels within the body, between two body parts (you can initially suggest them; e.g., shoulder and hip). Then, dancers send pulses along an unexpected pathway through the body (e.g., into the knee or around the ribs twice).

3. To help dancers achieve the best possible movement quality, ask them to imagine the pulse as something tangible, such as a ball, moving in the body.

One dancer directs energy out of an elbow and to another dancer.

4. Ask dancers to explore how impulses flow along different pathways through the body. Remind them to make their movements fluid and natural.

5. Now, have dancers send signals to each other: One dancer sends the pulse through the body and out of a body part that is directed across the circle to another dancer, as if throwing out a ball of energy to be caught by another dancer. Each signalling dancer must be clear about the direction of movement so that the receiving dancer is aware of it; this may require looking at the receiver before passing the movement. Ask the receiving dancers to catch the signal in one part of the body, send it through as many body parts as they can and then throw it out of another body part to another dancer.

6. Dancers can pass the energy pulse until everyone has had a chance to receive and pass it. This exercise can be short in duration, or you can extend it if the dancers want to experiment and explore further.

Teaching Tip

If your group is large, keep in mind that they will be standing still while watching one dancer move and pass at a time. This gives them a chance to observe, but not to stay moving. To keep more dancers moving at once and to speed up the exercise, you can introduce the concept to the whole group in one large circle and then break them into smaller circles or other formations.

Further Development

Another way to explore this exercise is to change the dynamic of the pulse: Describe it as hot or erratic or made of light shining through the body. You can set up a more structured improvisation by requiring that the signal pass through a specific body part of even multiple body parts at the same time. You can follow this improvisation with Signals and Pulses (page 44).

Different Quadrants

This improvisation challenges dancers to think about defining space and to consider that different actions can take place in different spaces. They will have the opportunity to start thinking for themselves, especially if they end up alone in one section of one of the defined spaces.

1. To get dancers moving through the whole space, ask them to create their own personal pathways by walking, running and galloping. You may give them ideas about the shape these pathways take (e.g., curved and then straight).

2. Next, divide the dance studio into four quadrants. Explain that when the dancers stop in each quadrant, they will perform different actions assigned to each quadrant. Some suggested actions are slow jumping, gestures with balances, turns at all three levels, stopping and starting swing actions, drawing one's own name with a body part or expressing different emotions. You or the dancers can decide the actions.

Dancers use balance, the floor, swinging and emotion in each quadrant.

3. Ask the dancers to travel as in step 1. On a given verbal cue (e.g., "Stop") the dancers stop, discover which quadrant they are in and perform the appropriate action.

4. When this exercise is successful, ask dancers in two of the quadrants to stop and observe the two other quadrants. For example, all the upstage dancers watch the downstage dancers and swap over taking turns to watch each other.

5. Have dancers travel again around the space, this time making more demands on what they do to create more interesting ways of travelling. Unless you want them to end up in the same quadrant, remind them that they can use the whole space. To increase demands, create new, more complex improvisation ideas for each space. For example: If you end up in the downstage right section, you have to create floor work that never stops; if you end up in the upstage left section you have to keep jumping but never repeat an action; whoever is in that space has to pass a movement to each other, each time adding on a new movement.

Teaching Tip

If dancers' movements become too simple or too difficult, you can give them more specific instructions for their actions. Some of the dancers may end up in the same quadrant because they have already worked out what movements they will perform. Encourage these dancers to stay in the moment by adding commands for changes of direction. You can simply say, "Stop; change direction; go."

Further Development

You can use the movement ideas in the quadrants to introduce a theme that you may want to develop. For example, you could develop the signals theme or the beginning of contact work. You can have set movement material for one part of the room that travels to another part of the room. You can divide the space in many different ways to create a more complex landscape. It could be the beginning of a chance-based piece of dance with musical cues and learnt phrases performed in each area.

Five Curves

This improvisation asks dancers to explore the five positions of the spine that are associated with Cunningham technique and see what else can happen with the body at the same time.

1. Ask the dancers to identify the curves that the spine performs in contemporary dance. In Cunningham technique the spine hyperextends, flexes forwards, flexes laterally and can form into one C-shaped curve. The five positions of the back are upright, curve, arch, twist and tilt. You or your dancers can draw these positions with stick figures.

2. Go over the arm lines used in the Cunningham technique (first, second, third, fourth and fifth position—the same positions used in ballet) and correct dancers in these shapes as they perform them.

Dancers demonstrate curves of the spine. Dancers must be warmed up before doing this improvisation task.

3. Next, ask each dancer to investigate which arm position could go with which curve or position of the spine. They can play with these positions on their own, in pairs or in small groups. Try giving them some of these instructions:

- ⚘ Stand upright with the arms in first position, hyperextend the spine and then open the arms to second position.
- ⚘ Try performing a lateral flexion and keep your arms in second; what happens? (It becomes a tilt.)
- ⚘ Stand with the arms in third position and add side curves. Try lunging in this shape.

- Stand with the arms and feet in first position, then curve the spine into a C shape.
- Flex forwards with arms in fourth position.

4. Ask the dancers to put several of these experiments together to make either a spine exercise or a phrase, finding a way to link the arms together.

5. Next, ask the dancers to add the background of the body (e.g., plié in second position, lunge and tilt, feet in fourth position, a triplet, a jump or any way of travelling). Here is a short list of ideas:

- Plié (bend both knees in any position)
- Lunge (one leg is straight and the other is bent)
- Fondu (balance on one bent leg)
- Any elevation or aerial step: jump or sauté (two feet to two feet), hop or temps levé (one foot to same), leap or jeté (one foot to the other foot), assemblé (one foot to two feet) and sissonne (two feet to one foot)
- Repeating triplet steps (down, up, up)

6. Ask dancers to form pairs or trios and create a short travelling phrase. They can use the short spine sequence that they have already created or create a new one that takes travelling into consideration.

7. Dancers can show their phrases to the rest of the class or to another pair or trio.

Teaching Tip

For best results, repeat this improvisation and accumulate movements over time so that the dancers get used to the spine positions first before adding feet and arms.

Further Development

Invite dancers to watch a Merce Cunningham dance piece and observe which curves and arm lines are used together. Have them note what else is happening with the body (e.g., is a triplet being formed?). After discussing their observations, you can repeat the improvisation and perhaps develop it further using the new movements that they have discovered.

Circle Dircle

This is a quick warm-up improvisation for new and younger groups. It asks dancers to respond quickly to the leader's directions whilst thinking about space and how they are travelling. It is a fun way to raise the heart rate and build stamina. Use it at or near the beginning of a session to get your dancers moving together as a community.

1. Ask the dancers to find a space in a circle, making sure that they are the same distance from the person on the left and the person on the right. The circle must be as big as possible and dancers must maintain this size throughout the improvisation. You do not have to enter the circle but your presence can be helpful to add clarity.

2. Have the dancers embark on a circular journey by walking clockwise. Let them know that they need to respond quickly to a set of given directions: walk, run, gallop, change direction, walk backwards, run backwards and stop. You can call out these directions randomly. Be sure to say "Stop" before each travelling command and keep the circle from getting smaller.

3. Once the group is comfortable with the activity and can maintain the size of the circle, you can give the command, "Go." When dancers hear this command they must run as fast as they can towards the person in front of them and see if they can tag the person without getting tagged themselves. Even after being tagged, they must keep the circle going. Once a dancer has been touched on the shoulder they must raise their arms until all the dancers' arms are in the air.

4. This exercise is challenging and may not work the first time. If it doesn't work, have the dancers try it again. You can try the exercise with two circles next to each other to make it more manageable for the dancers. If it does work, after the dancers' arms are all in the air, you can start again with a new set of commands.

Teaching Tip

If you have a big group or have tried this improvisation before, try using two circles that travel in opposite directions, one inside the other. Both the circles could race to see who can raise all their arms up first.

Further Development

To add interest to this improvisation, add new commands such as different ways to travel or different body parts to tag, or have the group form different shapes other than a circle. You can use some commands that allow dancers more choices and others that challenge them within those choices. For example, have them travel on their own pathway but then instruct them to stop and change direction.

How Many Body Parts?

You can use this improvisation as a warm-up for many of the improvisations in the book. It is a quick way to get dancers to work in groups. It gets them moving in the space with an awareness of where the other dancers are.

1. Ask the dancers to walk around the room anywhere they want to go. Encourage them to be creative and careful with the pathway that they are making; they can make curves and straight lines whilst paying attention to where the other dancers are so that they do not bump into them.

2. As they travel, give them a series of commands such as walk, run, gallop, change direction, travel in a straight line, travel backwards, stop or jog on the spot.

3. Next, ask them to form groups of a given number with a given number of body parts touching the floor for that whole group. For example, groups of 4 dancers have 24 of their body parts in contact with the floor. Once they can achieve this goal, they can go back to walking around the space as before.

Three dancers use two body parts to touch the floor.

4. Then, add more commands as they travel. For example, low levels work well for this task. Also, try having dancers dodge around each other or not let others pass them by.

5. Again, give them a number of group members and a number of body parts that they can have on the floor, making it more challenging each time. For example, have them try 3 dancers and 2 body parts; then 6 dancers and 3 body parts; then 2 dancers and 14 body parts. Have them travel on their own between each try.

6. To add another challenge, require that the number of body parts touch each other. This time, the more body parts that are involved, the harder it is to succeed.

7. Now, combine both challenges: The dancers must quickly form groups of a certain number, have a number or body parts in contact with the floor and a number of body parts in contact with other dancers. For example, try groups of three with two body parts on the floor and four body parts touching each other. This combination is challenging, but eventually dancers come up with an appropriate answer.

Teaching Tip

Encourage dancers to learn anatomy: Use the names of bones and muscles for body parts or have them tell you the correct anatomy terms for the parts they are using.

Further Development

For dancers who are familiar with each other, develop phrases using step 7 of the improvisation. How they get into and out of the final position could create an interesting phrase with dancers pushing, nudging, catching and responding into the shape as well as out of the shape.

Introduce the Space

You can use this improvisation as a warm-up before many of the improvisations in the book. It gets dancers moving in the space with an awareness of where other dancers are.

1. Ask the dancers to walk around the room anywhere they want to go. As they walk, ask them to pay attention to how they are walking: What kind of contact do the feet have with the floor? Are the arms swinging? Encourage them to be creative and careful with the pathway that they are making; they can make curves and straight lines whilst paying attention to where the other dancers are so that they do not bump into them.

2. As they travel, give dancers a series of commands, such as walk, run, gallop, change direction, travel in a straight line, travel backwards, stop or jog on the spot.

3. Whilst they travel, ask them to think of another dancer in the room and be aware of where that dancer is in the space without letting that dancer know. Ask them to think of a space in the room (e.g., in the centre at a low level). When you say, "Go," the dancers must persuade the person they have thought of into the space that they have picked. Initially they may try to do it verbally or they may be more forceful with each other. As they gain more experience, their actions become more subtle.

Dancers try to get another dancer into a space.

4. Next, have the dancers around the room again, making sure that they don't all start walking in one direction. Give the simple commands again and ask them to think of a new person and a new space. This time, the dancers must get their chosen person in the space and try to keep them there so they cannot move. Remind the dancers being kept in a space that they too must try to fulfil their objective of getting another dancer they had visualised into a space and to find a way to do it. This can often continue for a while and produce interesting moments if dancers can free themselves to pursue their chosen person.

5. For an advanced improvisation repeat the exercise, this time asking dancers to pick a body part of another dancer to put in a space at a certain level. You could repeat it again and have the dancers put two other dancers into a space and keep them there. Some groups may start picking each other up to move them to the space.

6. Next, try breaking the whole group into smaller groups. Ask each group to come up with a space, a level and a body part of every dancer they will put and keep in a space. This is a good time to use lifts, counterbalances and other contact moments; if dancers are too forceful, set some boundaries.

7. Ask the dancers to repeat the movements they did and work on the timing of each action, then repeat the movements until they become a fluid dance.

8. Ask the groups to share their work with the other groups and discuss what worked. You can add music for this part of the task.

Teaching Tip

To help this improvisation work more efficiently, be sure dancers know proper terms for the parts of the space (upstage, centre stage, downstage, stage right, stage left). Be sure that they understand the concept of low, middle and high levels.

Further Development

These movements can lead into small group dance pieces. Record the dancers on video and observe the movements. Choose effective movements to develop into phrases.

Pass the Movement

This is a short warm-up game that asks dancers to consider how a single movement that they have only seen but not performed, can be translated into their own bodies. It helps develop their observation skills and helps them learn how different dancers interpret movements they have seen. They have to think about size, level, time, correct action and which side of the body faces which part of the space. This improvisation works well at the beginning of a workshop to get all the dancers into the space and listen to direction as well as develop their movement memory and ability to copy movement.

1. Ask the dancers to form a large circle in the space. To ensure that dancers are evenly spaced, ask them to be the same distance from the dancer on their right as from the dancer on their left. You, too, must be part of the circle.

2. Ask the dancers to copy a movement that is passed to them from the person next to them. You may need to start the first movement; demonstrate it to the person next to you and send it around the circle. Each dancer must watch only the movement that is presented to them, then copy it and pass it on to the next dancer.

One dancer jumps after the movement has been shown to her.

3. When the movement has been passed around the entire circle, compare what it looked like when it started and how much or how little it has changed.

4. Try it again; this time a different dancer initiates the movement.

5. For an added challenge, ask dancers to keep their eyes closed until the person next to them taps them on the shoulder to show the movement. Then, once they have passed it on, they can observe how it is changing.

Teaching Tip

As dancers become more familiar with the task and develop their skills, you may add more movements, building from one to four or five.

Further Development

To hone observation and copying skills, have dancers work in pairs or small groups. Partners perform short movements or phrases for each other and try to get them to look the same.

Mirror or Follow

This improvisation gets dancers to disseminate, learn and remember movement material. They must consider which side of the body is in use and watch carefully to copy exactly the content of the actions performed. This exercise is great for bonding a pair or group before a performance, especially if they need to perform in unison.

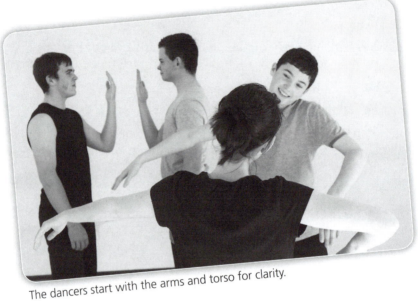

The dancers start with the arms and torso for clarity.

1. Have dancers find a partner. You can use groups of three if needed.

2. Ask the dancers to face each other and decide who is a dancer and who is the mirror.

3. The dancers must experiment with movement and see if their partner can copy it directly and simultaneously. At this point you can lead a discussion about what movements, levels, timings or directions the mirror can follow and what proves to be more difficult. Can the two dancers move in unison?

4. Have the dancers reverse roles. You can further challenge the dancers by asking them to change levels and try to travel.

5. Have each pair perform for another pair and ask the question, Who is the mirror? If they work very well as a pair, the answer may not be obvious.

6. The dancers can find another partner or stay with the original partner. The next step is to mirror and dance, dance and mirror, swapping roles over as many times as they can whilst they move around the room without talking. The pair should appear to be moving in unison.

7. Next, have the dancers find another partner and embark on a simple follow the leader task. You may need to give them body actions and other commands to create interesting movement material. Remind dancers that one partner can be slightly behind the other as they move in canon and they can use the same side of the body as each other.

8. Have the dancers swap roles again.

9. The final goal is to have the pairs mirror and follow without communicating any signals. You may see that one dancer moves across the room and the other stays behind because they both assume the leader role. In this case, they need to compromise.

10. Have the pairs perform their movements for the whole group.

Teaching Tip

It is a good idea to encourage discussion after each part of the task so that dancers can talk about what is working well. After the final performance to the whole group, try focusing the discussion on which actions were in unison and which ones created canon moments.

Further Development

This improvisation could lead into Keep the Shape (page 72). The dancers may have produced some interesting movements that can form the basis for a duet that incorporates unison and canon. This task does not consider the timing or dynamics used, so you can consider these concepts while developing phrases. You could also have dancers try Intention Invention (page 163).

Statues and Speed

This improvisation is a good way to encourage dancers to be aware of each other and the potential that they have to interact. This task raises awareness of the use of space by creating shapes or tableaux responding to where other dancers have positioned themselves in the space.

Dancers create a whole group statue.

1. Have dancers warm up using a warm-up game or technical exercises. If needed, explain or review the concepts of levels and planes.

2. Ask the dancers to form a large circle in the space. To ensure that dancers are evenly spaced, ask them to be the same distance from the dancer on their right as from the dancer on their left. The circle needs to be as big as possible so that the space in the middle is big enough to dance in.

3. Ask the dancers to go in the circle, one after another, to create a shape with their bodies that they can maintain for a while whilst the other dancers join them. Each dancer who enters the circle must create a new statue that complements the shape that is gradually being created. They can look at it from any angle, but try not to give

the dancers too much time to think about it. You may want to repeat this step with some key feedback to the group about using different levels, finding spaces to fill and making the shape interesting to an audience.

4. Next, organise the dancers into groups or four or five; each dancer in the group is a number from 1 to 4 or 5.

5. Ask the dancers to again create statues but this time only relating to the other dancers in their small group. Call out the numbers to get dancers to enter the circle. You may repeat numbers in different orders to keep the dancers alert. The dancers initially create a group tableau and then come out of their position when their number is called, re-assess and quickly find a new shape that complements the group before the next number is called.

6. To train dancers to respond more quickly, call out the numbers in any order and with varying time gaps between them.

7. Next, let the group decide when the shape shifts without the calling of numbers so that the tableau keeps evolving.

Teaching Tip

At first the dancers may find a shape with simple poses such as stands or lunges. To inspire their creativity, try showing them a few other shapes that they can use at various levels when they try the exercise again. Ideas include laying on the floor, making contact with another dancer, linking through another dancer's arms or legs or being closer to another dancer.

Further Development

To develop the shapes into more sophisticated movements, ask the dancers to find different ways to get into and out of each shape. For example, they can turn out of the shape, keeping all motions fluid so that the shape itself appears to dance.

Just Plain Running

This improvisation works well in large gym spaces. It warms up the body and gets dancers thinking about travelling across space whilst they create new movement material. Dancers can do this exercise in pairs. Remind them to be aware of other dancers in the space so that they don't collide.

The dancers need to be aware of each other and the space.

1. Ask the dancers to travel around the room, first galloping and then running, being aware of their pathways.

2. Ask the dancers to run as fast as they can, then as slowly as they can, using all available space in the room.

3. Try having dancers compete in a slow running race from one end of the room to the other; the dancer who comes in last, wins. You can add ideas such as running slowly whilst performing fast gestures and isolations. You can also have a fast running race that involves a slow ending.

4. Next, ask the dancers to run across the room to the beat of a 4/4 piece of upbeat music. You can develop it into pairs running corner to corner as you would in a technique class. You can play with run-

ning forwards and backwards but still covering the same amount of ground; for example, dancers do four runs forwards and four runs backwards on a straight line; both dancers turn the same way in the transition.

5. Ask the dancers to travel to the beat of the music in pairs, running from one side of the room to the other. Then ask them to add these three things, in any order: run side-by-side in unison, cross over pathways and run around each other. Dancers may have to vary their running speeds, especially to safely get around their partners.

6. Have each pair show this short sequence to the rest of the group.

7. Next, have dancers add in a moment when they are holding hands. Have them use each other's weight either as a quick counterbalance (e.g., right arm to right arm or both lean back in a squat and pull each other up) or as a support (e.g., one dancer stays still and pulls the other who is running around, or one pulls the other past them, or one supports the other on the floor and spins them on their back or pulls them up quickly into a jump). Remember with pulling or pushing a partner, sudden movements or ones that are unexpected can cause injuries. If dancers are unsure, ask them to slow down the action to see if there are any complications. Try these ideas and ideas of your own. Remember, the exploration requires that the momentum of the running dynamic doesn't stop.

8. Finally, ask the dancers to add in the gestures or movements from one or more sports. Some dancers will produce movements that really work; you may decide to put groups together to share movement material.

9. Dancers can show their travelling sequence to the music and their peers can guess the sports represented in the piece.

Teaching Tip

Before this improvisation, you may want to do a session that explores what dancers can do when they have contact with a partner. For example, when contact is with one hand, can they pull, push, lean, counterbalance and so on?

Further Development

You can use this improvisation as the entrance or exit to a dance piece. You can use it as the basis for whole group piece about sports or you can add anything that you are working on to part 8. You can also have dancers try the running in a zigzag pathway to a piece of music in 3/4 time.

Touch the Floor

This warm-up improvisation gets dancers to use their brains and bodies; they have to think about travelling in the space whilst quickly reacting to instructions. You can use this improvisation instead of Introduce the Space (page 56).

The dancers make quick contact with the floor.

   1. Ask the dancers to travel around the space, weaving in and out of the other dancers and making sure that they have been everywhere in the room as they travel.

   2. As the dancers travel through the space, ask them to do simple tasks that they have to execute immediately. Here are a few to get you started:

a. Walk	h. Touch the ceiling
b. Stop	i. Touch the floor
c. Go	j. Jump
d. Run	k. Roll
e. Change direction	l. Fast
f. Forwards	m. Slow
g. Backwards	n. Fall

3. If you use this improvisation warm-up again, you can add in many more things movements, exercises that you have performed in class or even give the dancers the opportunity to shout out a few commands themselves.

4. To get the dancers thinking quickly, change the consequence of the action you are shouting out. For example, try asking them to do the opposite movement: Stop means go, forwards means backwards, touch the ceiling is now touch the floor and so on. Try to challenge them by saying a few in a row: A command of "Go" followed by another "Go" usually gets at least one dancer moving.

Teaching Tip

This exercise works well with dancers at all levels and ages. You may want to have fewer commands at first and then layer more on when you do it again. You can use this exercise again many times.

Further Development

The dancers could create new commands in groups and then take turns shouting them out to the other dancers in the whole group. Several groups could be moving in the space at once; on a given command said by anyone in the room at any time, they could come together to do the same action or make a tableau. For example, someone shouts out, "Tableau" and the group quickly makes a shape together.

Work, Work and All Play

This improvisation could be an initial improvisation to get dancers to be aware of each other and increase the potential for them to interact. The key features involved are the use of gesture, rhythm, facial expression and timing. This is a fun session.

1. Have the dancers warm up with a warm-up game or technical exercises before doing this improvisation.

2. Ask the dancers to form a large circle in the space. To ensure that dancers are evenly spaced, ask them to be the same distance from the dancer on their right as from the dancer on their left. The circle needs to be as big as possible so that the space in the middle is big enough to dance in.

3. Put on a piece of upbeat music in 4/4 time and ask the dancers to go in the circle one after another to create a machine with their bodies. Dancers perform three different simple movements to the music. The sequence needs to be something they can maintain for a while whilst the other dancers join them. Each dancer who enters the circle must create a part of the machine that relates and complements the moving shape that is gradually being created. They can look at it from any angle, but try not to give them too much time to think about it.

One by one, the dancers add on to the machine.

4. You may want to repeat this exercise after giving the group some key feedback about using different levels, finding spaces to fill, using noises with the movements and making the shape interesting to an audience. The dancers may even be able to make contact with each other so that one action creates a reaction.

5. The next step is to organise the dancers into groups of four or five.

6. Ask the dancers to think of three different jobs (e.g., builder, hairdresser and doctor) and to create related pedestrian movements that use the music. Set a maximum number of counts per job so that they are restricted by time to get the jobs across.

7. Ask the dancers to think about creating movements that are in unison, canon, that accumulate and moments where each dancer is performing something different. They could also be inventive with the transitions from one job to another.

8. Allocate a short time for them to make their small group dance piece that incorporates three jobs.

9. Have groups perform for each other.

Teaching Tip

Finding a piece of music related to working, uses lyrics about working or has an industrial feel to it will further aid the dancers in producing interesting material.

Further Development

This improvisation is a good way to create group dance pieces. Ask the dancers to verbally describe their observations of what worked about the pieces they watched. One of the jobs could inspire the group to make a piece. You could use the initial pedestrian movement answers and explore choreographic devices to create exam or assessment pieces. If some of the movements created are memorable, consider using them for group warm-ups in the future.

Sign In

This exercise works well with new groups at the beginning of a session. It can also start the creative process for you to build on. Use it at any point in the term; it can produce interesting movement material that considers body parts in isolation. If groups are unsure about going into the circle try Five Seconds (page 38) first to help build confidence.

A dancer writes her name with her elbow.

1. Ask the dancers to form a large circle in the space. To ensure that dancers are evenly spaced, ask them to be the same distance from the dancer on their right as from the dancer on their left. You, too, must be part of the circle.

2. Ask the dancers to go into the circle one at a time and write their names in the space with a body part. Give them a few seconds to think which body part to use; depending on the dancers' abilities you may give them a few ideas either verbally or physically. Each dancer can write in the air or on the floor, as big or as small as they like.

3. One dancer enters the circle and signs in, then returns to the starting point. Then the next dancer in the circle has a turn. If you or the dancers are still learning their names, you can have them say their names before or after signing in.

4. Once everyone has signed in, you can see what types of movements they have chosen and where you may need to push ideas. Ask the dancers to go in to the circle to sign in again, maybe starting the other way around. This time the size of the movement is important: Ask the dancers to sign in as big as possible, perhaps including jumps and rolls with a different body part.

5. When you go around the circle again, try changing the body part, the size to small, the speed, the plane and anything else that you want to be considered.

6. Next, have dancers work in pairs. Ask them to create a motif that spells out their name but use a different body part for each letter. For example, use an arm for a D, the knee for an O, the head for an R and the hips for an A. Ask them to vary the speed, size, space, level and plane of each action.

7. Have dancers show their motifs to their partners for feedback; you could have them show the whole group if they are confident.

Teaching Tip

The dancers may want to sign in with a hand at first, so maybe ask that they pick another body part to challenge them. You could also try putting on different pieces of music to see how the dancers respond when they work on their own name motif.

Further Development

Dancers could learn each other's sequences or merge two together. You could also use A Recipe (page 165) at the end of the book to make group dance pieces as an introduction to how dance is structured. This exercise could lead into Body Part Conversation (page 106).

Keep the Shape

This improvisation is beneficial to new groups in a new space and helps dancers pay attention to where the other dancers are in the room. The students will be travelling and changing direction, so they must be aware of each other. You could use Just Plain Running (page 64) before this task.

1. Have all the dancers find a space in the room away from other dancers so that there are no gaps in the floor space.

2. The dancers can travel by running or walking around the space, making sure that the space has no areas without dancers.

3. To fill the space properly, signal the dancers to stop, then ask them to look around the space to see where the gaps are. Then, have them adjust where they are to fill these gaps.

4. Next, put the whole group into a formation; a triangle or rows of dancers can work well especially if one person is at the front. The leader can run anywhere in the room and stand with any facing and the rest of the dancers must quickly find the original formation and facing. If the leader just changed facing, all the other dancers would have to adjust where they are standing and facing.

5. The dancers can try any other formations that are more complex; perhaps they can face different directions and have different leaders each

Dancers keep a triangle formation.

time. They can then move one dancer around to a new space and facing in the room and all the other dancers have to adjust where they are around the central dancer.

6. Have the dancers try this task in smaller groups and again have them change leaders.

7. The next stage is to follow the leader of the group into the new space without discussing who the leader is. This means they have to swap roles frequently, so that in the time allotted they all have had a chance to be leaders. This improvisation is good practice for improvising where dancers have to pre-empt, respond and react with given movements.

Teaching Tip

Have the groups watch each other to see how differently they are doing it at any point.

Further Development

You could use this idea of changing where something is performed and where the movement should face with any movement material or group formations you have developed. So a sequence could frequently change facing and formation as well as where it is performed, which can add a fast-paced dynamic to the sequence.

4

MOVEMENT IMPROVISATIONS

This chapter contains improvisations that can lead to the creation of motifs, phrases and sequences to use with choreographic pieces or chapter 6, Developing Improvisations. Each improvisation in this chapter allows the dancer to consider one main aspect of choreography or a choreographic exploration to nurture and develop. Several tasks explore space, each from a different perspective: The Journey is about the space in the whole room, Encounters is about the space between dancers, Paint the Space is about personal space and Energy Impulses is about internal space. Other themes offered in this chapter are time, force, dynamics, rhythmic patterns and making shapes.

Paint the Space

This improvisation raises the heart rate and gets dancers to create short motifs. It starts in a circle and uses movements related to painting. You can use it as a warm-up at the beginning of class.

1. Ask the dancers to form a large circle in the space. To ensure that they are evenly spaced, ask them to be the same distance from the dancer on their right as from the dancer on their left.

2. Ask dancers to stand in a parallel or relaxed stance. Tell them to imagine that in front of them on the floor is a tray of paint in any colour of their choosing. Younger groups may want to tell you the colour.

3. First, have the dancers roll down through the spine until they can dip the top of the head into the paint. Ask them to paint a figure eight with the head, keeping in mind where the paint is going and picturing the image it leaves behind. This action helps to warm up the back and spine.

4. Next, have dancers place their hands in the paint and make patterns in the space around them on every level. You can ask them what colours they are using and whether they want to change colours. They may go to the obvious movement answer and place their hands on the floor, which can still create interesting movements if they explore more than just personal space.

5. Repeat steps 2 through 4 with different body parts to warm up the whole body. You can have dancers use personal space and general space.

6. Have dancers create movement phrases. An effective way to do this is to ask each dancer to put both their hands and feet into the paint and create a travelling pattern on the floor; they can use both hands and feet together and separately. Dancers need to remember the movements that they used to create this pattern.

One dancer makes a pattern with his hands and feet.

7. Once the dancers have a short phrase of around 5 to 10 movements, ask them to show a partner and make comments on what they thought was most effective. They must choose the movements that looked good to them and teach each other so that they can perform a unison phrase.

8. Repeat the exercise with groups of four dancers to make an even longer sequence.

Teaching Tip

When the dancers are creating their floor sequence with both hands and feet, see if they can turn, jump or travel across the floor. They may want to work in pairs to create this phrase.

Further Development

This is a great task for getting dancers to produce movement material at a low level. They can also mix in any other phrases of movements that they have created so that they start to go into and out of the floor level. You may also want to discuss how different colours (of paint in this case) may affect the quality or dynamics of the movements. You can use the sequences created in A Recipe (page 165).

Energy Impulses

This is an improvisation for pairs of dancers. It may be a further development from other tasks, such as Signal Circle (page 46) or Signals and Pulses (page 44). You can also use it on its own to create innovative phrases. It involves touch, so be wise about which groups you think could do it justice. It may not be appropriate for immature groups.

1. Ask the dancers to find a partner and a space in the room away from other dancers.

2. Explain that one dancer is the energy and one is the memory. The energy dancer will push, pull, poke, grab, pick up or drop the other's body parts in a sequence of five different things. For example, a dancer might push a shoulder down, pull the hips back, pull the arm up, poke the back of the knee forward and push the head down. Ask the dancers to try this with a different force each time (e.g., soft, hard, forceful, tender).

3. The memory dancer must remember how the energy impulses felt. Then, without the energy partner's touch, try to re-create the movements in the same order with the same. You may need to start with 2 impulses so that it is easier to remember. Have them try this several times.

4. Have the dancers switch roles so that they both end up with a phrase that has been created in this way. Some dancers find it easier to re-create the dynamics and quality of the movements with the eyes closed.

Dancers in pairs respond to their partner's touch.

5. Have dancers show their work to the rest of the group. Some dancers have a good grasp on the idea of finding quality in the movement from the force that created it; others can learn by observing them. At this point you can have dancers repeat the exercise with a new partner, using what they learned from the first experience.

Teaching Tip

When the memory dancer responds to the touch, no movement answer is wrong. The dancer may be pushed forward and then gravity may bring the body back, or pushed forward and stay forward. Dancers could try both responses.

Further Development

If you have not already tried Signal Circle (page 46), and Signals and Pulses (page 44), try them now. You may find that the dancers are now more open to the notion of passing energy through the body and can do those tasks in more interesting ways.

Disjointed

Dancers are to try this improvisation on their own, because they will explore the movements that their own arms and legs can do. The dancers will observe and perform for each other, then make choices about what they think is effective from the perspective of the observer and performer. This task encourages some consideration and appreciation skills and will open up conversation and discussion.

1. Ask the dancers to find a space in the dance studio with any facing. Have them explore the movement that the arms can do. Use commands such as "Flex, Extend, Rotate, How far can you reach?, What size circle can you make?, Swing and Can you lead the movement with the elbow?". Encourage dancers to create movements that are unlike anyone else's.

2. Then, have the dancers choose the movements that worked best and join them together to make a phrase of movement just for the arms. So, they will use the process of selecting and refining their movement material. This could include three movements or, if dancers are in a creative mood, it could be longer.

One dancer explores the movement possibilities of her arms.

3. Have the dancers face a preselected partner or anyone near to them in the space, then show their arm sequences. Then have the dancers share feedback based on two key observations, such as use of space or any meaning that they thought the movements had.

4. Next, have dancers repeat the exercise, this time exploring the movement potential of the legs and creating a phrase for the legs only. Remember, legs can travel.

5. Have dancers share their leg phrases, this time with a different partner. Ask them again to share feedback using two observations; it could be as simple as two things they liked and why.

6. Next, have dancers put together the arm and leg phrases. Here are some ideas to try:

    ⑥ **Disjointed:** The movement material does not easily go together; it may look out of control.

    ⑥ **Harmonious:** They may complement each other or one movement might be the impulse for another. Dancers could have two sequences here or pick just one.

7. Have dancers share their work in larger groups and comment on whether it was effective, what worked and what they would do differently if they did it again.

Teaching Tip

You may want to take a sequence that the whole class already knows. They could perform the arms from one sequence and legs from another. Then they can experiment with the ideas of disjointed and harmonious compositions before adding the challenge of creating their own material to do it with. More experienced dancers could try creating phrases to a certain rhythm or piece of music.

Further Development

You can have students experiment with different pieces of music for the same set of sequences. The material could be taught to everyone to create a small group or whole group piece.

Time

This exercise will challenge students' concepts of time, how it is individually experienced, how this compares to other dancers and how it can be used to create and refine movement material to produce interesting phrasing and high points.

1. Ask the dancers these questions: How long can you do one movement for? As a spectator, how long would you want a piece of dance to last in a performance and why? How many movements can you do in 1 second?

2. Ask the dancers to use the entire dance space. Have them walk around, creating pathways that weave around the other dancers and around the room. When these pathways have been established, ask the dancers to walk for 1 minute without counting, looking at a clock or looking at a watch. Ask them to stop walking when they think the minute has come to an end. Remember the time of the first person that stopped and the last so you can draw their attention to how much the concept of time differs from person to person.

Dancers explore moving at a fast pace.

3. This time, have dancers run at a fast pace around the room for what they perceive is 1 minute. When they have all stopped, compare the length of the estimated minutes once more and see if they are longer or shorter than the estimated minutes during the walking exercise. So, was their walking minute less or more than their running minute? Ask the dancers why this may be.

4. Ask the dancers to find a space separate from other dancers. Instruct them to perform every dance or athletic movement that they have ever done or seen to prompt them to perform as many different dance movements as they can. Tell them to use as much space as they need but only to perform over a period of 15 seconds that you time. If dancers repeat movements or don't manage to move fast enough, try the task again, this time giving directions that encourage rapid movement.

5. Have dancers play with the concept of fast movement by performing as many movements as they possibly can within different time limits such as 5 seconds, 20 seconds and 7 seconds. ("Do as many movements as you can in 5 seconds; ready, go: 1, 2, 3, 4, 5 stop.")

6. Repeat the exercise, this time experimenting with the size of the movements they perform to see if the dynamics vary. For example, dancers could perform as many large movements as they can in 10 seconds.

7. Repeat the exercise, but don't tell them how much time was allocated. For example, give them 7 seconds to perform as many movements as they can that are all different, then ask each dancer to guess how long they were dancing. Observe the various answers and concepts of time.

8. Next, ask the dancers to find a partner to whom they will perform one simple movement. You have prepared this movement for them before the session. It is best to keep the movement simple. For example, start with the arms crossed in front of the chest, then opening out to the side to end in second position. Have the dancers demonstrate the movement as slowly as they can.

9. Whilst dancers watch their partners ask them questions to think about. For example, "At what point do you lose interest in watching your partner? Why? How does this relate to time? What would the movement look like if it was filmed and sped up? Would it be smooth?"

10. Have dancers switch roles; the performer becomes the audience and the audience becomes the performer. Once all dancers are finished, collect the answers to the questions that you asked. Then

ask, "Why can slow movement switch an audience off? How can one keep them on the edge of their seats—or at least awake?"

11. Give the dancers a simple phrase of movement that they play with in terms of time; they will allocate time to each movement or fragment of movement. Give the task itself a time limit. For example, allocate 1 minute to play and refine the sequence. Ask the dancers to give a surprising variation of their chosen timings. Encourage multiple changes of tempo and speed of movement so that every dancer has a different speed for every movement. This is a good time to express the importance of breath in making movements seem fast.

12. If you have more class time, ask the dancers to add on four of their own movements, maybe body actions that are not in the initial phrase. They must experiment with both time and dynamics by using very fast movements that interrupt slow movements so that they can surprise the audience. Encourage them to experiment with their breathing.

13. Place groups of dancers together in the space to perform their phrases. Ask the audience where they would position the performers using interesting formations; this encourages them to consider the visual effect. After the performance, have the group discuss what aspects worked well. For example, ask, "What movements stood out? How does the concept of time change the dynamic?"

Teaching Tip

Hide all the clocks and watches in the room before you start.

Further Development

Have students watch some dance pieces that play with time. Here are some good choices:

- ⊚ *Rush* (by Akram Khan)
- ⊚ *Rosas* (by Anna De Keersmaeker)
- ⊚ *Vespers* (by Ulysses Dove of the Alvin Ailey Dance Company)
- ⊚ *Constant Speed* (by Mark Baldwin of Rambert Dance Company)
- ⊚ *Stand and Stare* (by Darshan Singh Bhuller for Rambert Dance Company)

Dancers can use the phrases they created with any of the tasks in chapter 6 of this book.

Elastic Force

This improvisation explores the idea of being tugged by an elastic force. This force can be between body parts or from different sides of the room or attached to a space. Before doing this exercise, warm up dancers with a warm-up game or technical exercises.

1. Ask the dancers to stand away from other dancers and imagine that there is an invisible piece of elastic between their hands. Ask them what might happen if they try to open the arms wide. Have them show you what the movement looks like.

2. Ask them to play with having elastic between other given body parts (e.g., head and foot) and think about the change in dynamics (speed, force) between the pulling apart and the coming back together. Then, ask them to choose their own two body parts to explore. If dancers struggle to come up with more than one movement answer for each body part, you may need to call out different body parts to keep them working positively. Particularly creative groups may explore the movement potential further by involving travelling and perhaps levels.

3. Have the dancers work in pairs and show each other the movements that they came up with (or, if they struggle to remember the movements, the basic improvisation idea).

4. Now, have partners explore having elastic between each other's body parts. You may want to start with hands: one hand, then both hands. Then, have dancers change the distance between them to encourage travel and floor work.

Two dancers pull with an imagined elastic attached to their hands.

5. Have the dancers work in groups of four or more share what they came up with. Have the dancers in each group learn each other's individual phrases and use them to create a large group sequence. Then, if the pieces and the dancers are ready, have them perform their sequences to other groups and end with a discussion.

Teaching Tip

Young groups may want to have an actual piece of elastic to work with. The ideal size used in French skipping would be a piece around 3 metres long and 1 centimetre thick, and is joined to make a continuous loop. Both the dancers can then loop each end around a body part and begin exploring the possible movements.

Further Development

The dancers can set some of the movements that they come up with in the duets using their own phrases that they initially created. Some groups could add lifts of counterbalances at the rebound phase of the movement. They can further develop movement material by adding choreographic devices such as retrograde or making the movements smaller or faster.

Accumulation Nation

This improvisation introduces dancers to how movement can be phrased. It asks dancers to consider how a single movement that they have only seen once can be translated into their own bodies. Then, they must consider the weight, force and flow of that movement to add on another movement. Use this task to get dancers to come into the space and listen to directions. It can also develop movement memory, ability to copy movement. You can introduce it after Pass the Movement (page 58) or Just Plain Running (page 64). You can repeat this task many times, emphasising many topics.

All dancers follow the central dancer's actions.

1. Ask the dancers to form a large circle in the space. To ensure that dancers are evenly spaced, ask them to be the same distance from the dancer on their right as from the dancer on their left. You, too, must enter the circle.

2. Have yourself or one dancer create a movement and pass it to an adjacent dancer. Each dancer copies and passes the movement around the circle. When it has arrived back where it started, discuss whether dancers all used the same side of the body, rhythm and force to demonstrate the movement. Try it again with a different dancer starting and see if it can come full circle looking the same.

3. Next, have yourself or one dancer start a movement and pass it; this time, each dancer adds on another movement and demonstrates it for the next dancer in the circle. The movement will become a phrase and then a sequence. Have all dancers copy the phrase after each person adds to it so that they all know it and can perform it. As the phrase gets longer and longer, dancers must work harder to remember all the details, such as time, facing and size, correctly.

4. When the movement has been passed around once, it will be a long sequence. It may not work well in terms of being phrased (e.g., having high points or any variation). See how the dancers can solve phrasing problems, then give them directions for how to make it more fluid next time they perform it.

5. For the next phase, have dancers do the same task; this time, have them consciously explore how each added movement naturally follows the movement that has been given to them. As each dancer adds on, get them to think about where their weight is and what their body wants to do next as a logical progression. If the movement before is a balance, then the next movement has to be some kind of fall. Or, if the move before is a turn, the dancer must consider momentum to create the next movement. As the group accumulates movements this time, the phrasing should be more feasible.

6. Ask all of the dancers to face one direction, maybe to face the mirror if you have one, and perform the whole phrase. The timing and shape of the movements must be clear to all.

Teaching Tip

You may need to get the dancers to repeat the movements several times before adding another movement so that they really understand what movement could go next.

Further Development

You could put the dancers in small groups to explore and manipulate the movement material with either given or chosen choreographic devices to make a sequence. They could also think about unison, different types of canons, formations, making it travel or where a lift or contact moment might be. At the end, ask the groups of dancers to show their phrases to each other so that they can see how differently they have worked with the same movement phrase. For a good introduction to how to structure dance, use A Recipe (page 165) at the end of the book to make group dance pieces.

The Journey

This improvisation explores the space as a whole and allows each dancer to create a phrase of movement that travels. Before this task, warm up dancers with a warm-up game or technical exercises.

Dancers on their own journey.

1. Ask the dancers to walk around the room thinking about the trace that they make in the space as if they were being watched from above.

2. Ask them to create a pathway. Remind them that they can include straight lines, curves, zigzags, circles, triangles or other shapes. They must explore the entire space and end up where they started.

3. As they make the pathway they will encounter other dancers that they will either have to wait to pass or move around. Every time this happens, they must include the movement that they did even if next time they perform the pathway the other dancer is not there.

4. Repeat this idea of creating movement from encounters until dancers have accumulated more movement material. Add commands to expand the movement potential. For example, tell dancers that if they encounter each other they can perform any of these choices:

a. Go under them
b. Climb over them
c. Lift them out of the way
d. Jump to the side
e. Wait in a balance into a fall

Again, remind the dancers that when they repeat the pathway, they must perform the same movement at the same point—even lifting or moving under someone—even if this time around, the other dancer is not there.

5. Ask the dancers to work in pairs and perform their pathways for each other. Have them pick out moments that were interesting to watch, then share what they came up with. This gets dancers to select and refine their movement material. The duets could travel on their own pathways and learn parts of each other's movements that they can perform in unison. They could also pick out some of the initial encounter movements, such lifts or counterbalances, that they liked or that they think worked.

6. Ask the dancers to share their work with another pair and to then select and refine (edit) each other's duets to come up with a shorter and more interesting duet.

Teaching Tip

Young groups may want to design their journey on paper like a map before they start this task. Older groups may want to use an abstract painting to give them a pathway.

Further Development

Groups could watch the duets and discuss what works and why. Also, if you have a mature group who can be tactful, ask what doesn't work, why they think so and how they would change it. Encourage dancers to think creatively by asking what they would like to do with the duets to further develop them as performance pieces.

Jumping Jacks

You can use this improvisation task to create dynamic phrases of movement. You could do How Many Body Parts? (page 54) or Sign In (page 70) before this improvisation. Make sure that legs and feet have been warmed up for jumping with pliés, tendus, brushes or other appropriate warm-up exercises.

1. Ask the dancers to form a circle. Have them perform any jump that they can think of one by one around the circle. Remind them of the five different types of jumps: jump or sauté (two feet to two feet), hop or temps levé (one foot to the same foot), leap or jeté (one foot to the other foot), sissonne (two feet to one foot) and assemblé (one foot to two feet).

2. Ask the dancers to perform as many of the jumps that they remember seeing the other dancers perform in one go. Ask them why they think that they remembered the ones that they did.

3. This time around, have dancers perform jumps or aerial steps in a shape that have never been seen before. They need to be creative and come up with original material.

Dancers perform different types of jumps.

4. The dancers may need further assistance to encourage them to create innovative jumping actions. Ask them to consider if they are jumping upwards or along, if they are using leg or arm gestures and if they are inhaling to help the jump look more effective.

5. Ask the dancers to take turns using aerial steps to travel from the corner of the room. You can use music, which may help emphasise dynamics. If you have a large group or if the dancers can avoid each other and don't want to travel solo, they can do this in pairs.

6. The dancers then need to find a space in the room away from other dancers. Ask them to pick or create three different jumps and perform them with interesting arm and leg gestures. The next step is to find a way of moving or travelling into and out of each jump, which could include any other body actions. The last step is to try linking all three jumps together. They might go into and out of the floor to create another level; in this case, they need transitions. They need to remember this sequence to use later, so it may be a good idea to quickly share what they have created; half the group could perform for the other half, then switch. Encourage clapping at this stage. You may want to leave this improvisation here and develop the motifs that have been created.

7. Next, ask the dancers to pick one body part and play with how they can make that body part jump in three different ways. This may be an isolation type movement that has a quick, sharp dynamic. If the dancers find this difficult, ask them to put the three jumps they have created into the body part or tell them to imagine that the body part is a bouncing ball.

8. Ask them to experiment with several different body parts; you or they can decide which parts.

9. Finally, get them to use their entire finding, both the actual jumps and the body part jumps to create a short motif about bouncing. They can mix up the movements or put the aerial steps at the beginning or the end of the phrase.

10. Dancers can learn a lot by watching, so ask them to share their motif with a partner for feedback, editing, phrasing or adding.

Teaching Tip

Ask each group to create a focus pathway (looking at given points whilst performing the sequence) for each other as a way to refine and develop performance skills. A focus pathway helps the dancer express meaning in the work and helps the dancer avoid looking on the floor or around the room with no purpose. Dancers can do this facing front for nearly all, looking down so that the audience can focus on a body part or with the eyes following pathways, planes, actions or other dancers. Explain to your students that a dancer's direction of gaze whilst performing can add a layer of meaning or narrative to the performance. Where a dancer looks can change with every movement that is performed on stage. For example, ballet dancers often look at their partners in a pas de deux. In modern dance a dancer may not look at the audience for a sense of emotion, meaning or abstraction. If a dance piece is about a memory of another person, the dancer may look at a given space on stage as if they were there.

Further Development

For further investigation, dancers can perform the phrases to different pieces of music. For body part jumping, dancers can play with finding the same dynamic but jumping on the horizontal plane (sideways) as well as the sagittal plane (forwards and backwards). In terms of developing with choreographic devices, these sequences can often look effective when they start by accumulation and use retrograde. You can help dancers refine them and teach them to other dancers to create unison or canon sections of a dance piece.

Rhythm Is a Dancer

This improvisation is a great way to put some theory into practice. Before doing this task, have dancers warm up and be focused.

   1. Ask the dancers to get into small groups of three or four and remember a ring tone or song that they find themselves singing. Or, you could play a short piece of music for them to use.

   2. Ask the dancers to put this rhythm into their bodies quite simply by clapping, stamping or stepping the rhythm.

Four dancers clap out a rhythm.

   3. Next, have the dancers create a new rhythm that they can together initially clap and stamp in a 4/4 time signature using this idea of counts: 1 and a 2, 3 and 4, 5, 6, 7—miss 8. You can create your own rhythm or get the dancers to create a rhythm as a group. You may need to set the speed of the counts and have an expected duration.

   4. Get them to clap out loud and see if other groups can pick it up.

   5. Ask dancers to put the rhythms into their bodies using isolations, steps, turns, jumps and so on; each count is a different action.

   6. Ask the individuals to perform their phrases to the group. You could play with using different pieces of music to see how well things fit. If groups are working well together and are ready, the groups can perform for other groups, too.

Teaching Tip

Explain the value of bars and beats (most teachers count in 5,6,7,8). Explain whole counts (4 beats), half counts (2 beats), quarter counts (1 beat), eighth counts (1/2 beat) and sixteenth counts (1/4 beat). These can be on or off beats. If you have knowledge of the correct musical terms, you could start to introduce these in your descriptions. Ask the dancers to identify time signatures. Play them a waltz (3/4), a march (2/4) and any pop song in common time (4/4). Also discuss beats per minute (bpm); most popular songs are 120 bpm.

Further Development

You could do this task backwards as well by getting the dancers to clap the rhythm of a sequence or phrase performed in class. Then, turn that rhythm into a new phrase of movement. This idea of playing a rhythm with different body parts could lead into the Body Part Conversation (page 106) task. It could also develop into the Rhythm Nation (page 96) task.

Rhythm Nation

Dancers need be warm before having fun with this improvisation. You may also want to have some rhythms up your sleeve before you start the session. You can use this task to build on the Rhythm Is a Dancer (page 94) improvisation.

1. Ask each dancer to find a space in the dance studio away from other dancers.

2. Spend some time exploring rhythms and putting them into body parts. You can set rhythms by clapping, stamping, beating a drum and calling out a body part that needs to be moved with that rhythm. Dancers will come up with more interesting material if no two movements that they perform are the same or similar.

3. Ask the dancers to create a short phrase of movement based on a rhythm. These rhythms could come from ringtones or songs or they could use the rhythm of their name.

Two dancers use their rhythms together to complement each other.

Ask them to use at least three different body parts and more than one level.

4. When they have created a short phrase, ask dancers to share it with a partner. See if they can clap back the same rhythm to their partner from the phrase they are shown.

5. Then, ask the two dancers to set these two phrases together and experiment with the different ways to connect their timings. Dancers could start at different times and share each other's rhythms and movement material. They could move into the shapes or spaces that the partner creates or leaves behind.

6. Have the pairs show their work to the rest of the group. If dancers are not yet confident enough to show their work to the whole group, work with a smaller audience.

Teaching Tip

Even if you have only prepared a simple rhythmic pattern, it will still give the dancers the chance to explore. If you need help coming up with a pattern, try using a musical score or ask a music teacher to help with this session.

Further Development

Sometimes one or two duets have come up with some great ideas that peers could learn from. You could have them teach their movements to the other pairs. Another idea is to group pairs into fours and have each group of pairs share and learn each other's work. You can also have students repeat the interlocking with a new partner.

Space Race

This improvisation gets dancers to think about travelling in the space whilst creating movement material. They need to be able to work independently but be aware of where the other dancers are so that they don't collide. You could do Introduce the Space (page 56) first to prepare for this improvisation.

1. Ask the dancers to stand in their favourite space in the room, then stand in their least favourite space, then travel to a space that they are not really too bothered about.

2. Ask the dancers to create a pathway that links each of these three places in the room; the pathway must be more creative than just straight lines.

3. Have the dancers go to the first space and pick a body part to circle.

4. Then, have the dancers find a way to travel to the next space that is more than just

Dancers perform movements while creating pathways.

walking or running; dancers must remember what they are creating as they go.

5. Next, ask the dancers to perform a movement on a low level, finding a way into and out of the floor level in their second space. This must connect somehow to the way that they travelled to that space.

6. As they come out of the floor, ask them to link a new way of travelling to the last space. You may want to ask them to add a jump or a turn, but they must try something that is at a different speed from the first way of travelling.

7. When dancers reach the last space, ask them to perform a balance that suspends into a fall.

8. You can ask the dancers to repeat each section as they accumulate movements before you add on the next task. Ask the group to perform their space race; you may want to watch in two groups to allow for enough room and so that the dancers can watch each other.

Teaching Tip

You are asking the dancers to create and remember quite a lot in a short time frame, so you may ask then to rehearse what they have just created before they go onto the next step.

Further Development

The dancers can learn each other's space race in pairs or trios to create a longer unison travelling sequence. The dancers could work in groups of three or four to find moments that they meet on their travels, then create a greeting or parting action such as a lift or contact moment. It could be that they pause or have a moment of stillness whilst the other dancer passes or they copy that dancer's movements before continuing on their own pathway.

Take Three Shapes

This is a good individual improvisation that can use three salient positions from any piece of repertoire or from a dancer's previous choreography. It is especially helpful to dancers who struggle to choreograph their first motif or idea. This improvisation can work well with Signals and Pulses (page 44). Dancers will need to be warmed up before this task.

1. Ask dancers to find a space away from other dancers so that they are spread out.

2. Demonstrate in turn each of the shapes and salient positions shown here and ask the dancers to show them to you exactly. You can get them into pairs to work on perfecting the shape, or you can take positions from any dance piece. Dancers can come up with their own three shapes from research into their own choreography.

3. Ask the dancers to find a way into shape 1. They might have one body part leading, travel, go into the floor, jump or even push the body into the shape with other body parts.

4. Once they are in this shape, ask them to perform a quick gesture (non-weight-bearing action) so they can perhaps quickly move a foot, a hand, an arm, a knee, a leg or the head. They could even perform a facial expression.

5. Ask the dancers to find another original way of getting from shape 1 into shape 2. It could be from an energy that is passed through the body or a body part leading or suspension into a fast-moving falling action. Ask them to experiment with several ideas before they pick one.

6. Then ask dancers to get from shape 2 to shape 3. You could ask them to change dynamics or add a body action that you think is missing (e.g., a turn).

7. After a little rehearsal, the dancers should end up with a phrase of movement that passes through each shape. Ask them to keep it continuous and find which one point is the high point; have them use their breath to make the high point stand out.

8. Have dancers share their phrases and discuss them.

Teaching Tip

Ask the dancers to perform their phrases to music so that the sequence has a fluid feel to it. Dancers could also pick out the rhythm or instruments from the music with their movements.

Shape 1.

Shape 2.

Shape 3.

Further Development

Dancers can show their work to a partner. Together they can discuss the high point and whether any other points could be made more effective with in the use of breath, a bigger movement or a faster dynamic. Dancers can develop this motif using standard choreographic devices or any other ideas from chapter 6.

Restrictions

This improvisation explores the idea of having simple restrictions placed on the body and gives dancers the chance to explore new movements. Before this improvisation, have dancers do a warm-up. Try starting the session with This Is Me (page 25) or Space Race (page 98) to prepare dancers physically and mentally for the task ahead.

1. Ask the dancers to stand away from other dancers and imagine that one of their feet is stuck to the floor. They must explore this limit and try to reach out with body parts in all directions and levels. Try it again with the other foot so that the dancers use both sides.

2. Next, ask them to play with having one hand fixed to the floor; they can turn around, but the hand must not come off the floor. Encourage them to fully explore what they can do on the floor and which body parts they can move.

Dancers keep their hands fixed to the floor and experiment with the movements that can be performed from this point.

3. The dancers can now pick another body part of their choice to be fixed to the floor and explore the range of movements that can be performed from this point.

4. Ask dancers to choose three or four movements from the three quick improvisations that they explored. Ask them to put them together in any order.

5. Have dancers work together in pairs to show each other the movements that they came up with (or, if they struggled to remember the movements, the basic improvisation idea).

6. Now, have dancers explore what these two sequences would look like if they are put together. Dancers can move under, around, through or over their partners. They may change the timing, facing and level to fit in with their partner's movement. Partners may restrict each other, too.

7. Ask the dancers to perform their duets and discuss what worked with the whole group. Ask, "Were there moments of humour? Can facial expressions add or take away the clarity?"

Teaching Tip

You may want to have dancers stop after creating solo sequences and share them with the rest of the group. The dancers can learn at lot from watching their peers.

Further Development

Dancers can add manipulations or counterbalances into the duet. They can also travel. You could use the best moments from each duet to create a unison duet section in a whole group piece. The dancers could also explore being fixed in some way to their partner and explore the movement possibilities. The dancers could come up with a list of restrictions to use in other sessions. A few examples are included in RADS and Restrictions (page 150).

Body Actions

In this improvisation, dancers produce a travelling phrase that includes every body action. It helps dancers with their movement memory and gives them an interesting sequence that they can develop. Dancers could do Introduce the Space (page 56) or Touch the Floor (page 66) to warm up and prepare for this improvisation.

1. Ask the dancers to walk from one end of the room to the other in a straight line without colliding. If you have a large group, have dancers form lines of four or five. Once they have reached the other side of the room, they don't have to come back to the side that they started from but can regroup and travel back. This time, ask them to change the speed of walking and maybe even run at some point. Going across in lines gives dancers the opportunity to watch each other and learn from each other.

2. Once they have the idea that they are travelling from one side to the other at different speeds, have dancers find different ways to travel from the other dancers in their line. Once this has been established, you can begin the process of accumulating movements.

Dancers travel across the room.

3. First ask the dancers to find their own unique way of travelling; if they do something difficult to maintain or repeat such as walking on their hands, offer them the option to change it as they progress.

4. Have dancers use this way of travelling to travel back so that they remember what they have done. Explain that everything that they add on from here on, as they cross the room each time, needs to be remembered.

5. Ask the dancers to cross the room using their way of travelling and each time to add on a creative, original action. They can perform anywhere on the straight pathway, the beginning, the middle or the end. Here are some possible add-ons:

  a. Add a jump
  b. Add a turn
  c. Add a moment of stillness
  d. Add a gesture
  e. Add a balance
  f. Add a fall

6. Have dancers perform these sequences. Try having them perform in two groups crossing from each side of the room so that they can watch each other.

Teaching Tip

Give the dancers a chance to remember and perfect their movements as they add each action into their sequence.

Further Development

Dancers can use this material to create a chance piece in which they cross the stage at different times. If some moments stand out, you can teach them to all the dancers and use them for unison sections of whole group choreography or as a warm-up phrase in technique class. Dancers could use choreographic devices (e.g., changing the pathway of parts of the sequence) to further develop their material.

Body Part Conversation

This improvisation can lead to creating interesting duets. It gets dancers to respond to movements quickly with or without contact. Dancers must choose responses that are relevant to their partners' movements. Before doing this improvisation, dancers must be warmed up. They can do Sign In (page 70) to prepare for this improvisation.

In pairs, dancers respond and explore ways to communicate with body parts.

1. Ask the dancers to find a partner and a space in the room and sit on the floor back to back with the knees in front. Assign each dancer in the pair the role of either A or B.

2. Ask the dancers to tell a joke to their partner by only using their back and the contact that they have made with their partner. Partner A goes first whilst partner B makes sure that they don't bang backs to complete this task. Then they switch roles. Give them a chance to discuss this experience after they have told the joke. Did they get the idea that it was a joke from the types of movements?

3. Next, ask partners to tell each other a sad story or have an argument; they must do this part without harming each other.

4. Have the dancers stand up and face each other. This time, when they have a conversation they can see their partner and the movements they both perform. Ask the dancers to have a short conver-

sation but to use a different body part for each movement whilst considering the speed of the movement and spatial pattern. For example, they may circle an arm, step to the side, isolate a shoulder and wiggle their hips. Dancers will need to dance as if they are saying sentences; one person dances, and one listens and then responds.

5. After they have tried this you may need to give them more direction. The next phase is to point out that if they repeat movements that their partner has performed, it mirrors a conversation more accurately. For example, A says, "Are you going to the park?" and B says, "To the park? Yes, I may." The word *park* has been repeated so you would expect movement material to be repeated, too. Remind dancers that they must not rely only on repeating each other sentences, though. They may vary the lengths of their sentences, as long as one partner does not consistently use only short sentences.

6. Once they have got the idea you can then add another layer such as what type of conversation they are having. It could be asking directions (without actually pointing!), talking about the weather, having an argument, telling a funny story, explaining how something works, flirting or breaking up. You can suggest subjects, or have the dancers come up with their own. Encourage dancers not to do literal or obvious movements but rather rely on other ways to get their points across, such as quality, size, actions, dynamics and use of space.

7. If some dancers are working well together, ask them to demonstrate their conversations to the rest of the group and share ideas that all students can use.

8. Next, have students explore ways to add contact moments to the conversation.

9. If you desire, you can have dancers create short duets using the movements that they have used.

Teaching Tip

Dancers can swap partners and try working with other dancers in the group.

Further Development

The duets used could form part of a whole group piece or all dancers could learn one duet. If all duets have great moments, then dancers can join fragments of everyone's duets to create a unison duet section of a dance composition. This task could also lead into more contact improvisation tasks.

Puppet Strings

This improvisation gets dancers to think about travelling in the space whilst quickly reacting to instructions and other dancers. It could lead to developing interesting movement phrases. You could do Touch the Floor (page 66) to warm up the dancers and prepare them for this improvisation.

1. Ask the dancers to walk around the space weaving in and out of the other dancers and making sure that they have been everywhere in the room as they walk. Ask them to create interesting floor patterns as they go.

2. As the dancers walk, ask them to imagine that they are puppets and that they have strings attached to many body parts, which could be pulled at any point by an imaginary puppeteer.

3. Next, call out body parts that the puppeteer controls. For example, if you shout out, "Elbow," the dancers continue to travel around the room as if an imaginary force is pulling them by the elbow.

The dancers move as if they have strings attached to them.

Continue to call out more body parts one at a time to get dancers moving. Make sure that as they move, they don't all start travelling in a circle; remind them of their floor patterns.

4. The next step is to add on extras. When you call out a body part, also include a level and a speed or quality. For example, "Shoulder, low level, erratic." You can also add general directions. For example, "The puppeteer is pulling up, now down, now in a circle." You can have lots of fun with this part, adding on anything else that you think may work.

5. Next, ask the dancers to find partner. It could be the person nearest to them. They will take turns being the puppet and the puppeteer.

6. Ask them to stand facing each other. The puppeteer pulls imaginary strings from different body parts about 20 centimetres away. The trick is to move at the same speed as the hand pulling the string to look as if the string really exists. The dancers can decide if their body parts will stay where they are placed in space or drop back where they came from.

7. Have the dancers switch roles. Then, ask them if they can do the exercise again and see if the puppeteer can make the puppet walk.

8. The next step is the quest for a motif. Ask the dancers to move each other five times with strings, remember the movements with the same timing and perform them back to their partner. Ask both dancers in the pair to create a motif.

9. Dancers can then learn each other's motif, practise it and then finally show it to the rest of the group. Encourage the whole group to comment on what was effective about the movements and even what they might want to do with the motifs next.

Teaching Tip

Young groups may want to try this exercise with strings or look at how a real puppet may move and copy.

Further Development

The dancers could develop these motifs into phrases using choreographic devices. It could lead into more trust type exercises such as Clay Sculpting (page 124).

Retiré

This improvisation explores the idea of falling, tipping or tilting off balance from one supporting leg. Dancers need to be able to fall and recover with a mature approach to safety and be able to push their risk taking in off-balance positions to create interesting responses. Before doing this task, have the dancers warm up with a warm-up game or technical exercises.

The dancers at different stages of falling.

1. Ask the dancers to stand away from other dancers and balance on one leg. Then, have them try with the other leg and see how long they can stay there. Ask the dancers if they can balance better on their left or right leg.

2. Show the dancers retiré (foot to knee) position with the toe touching the knee in parallel and turned-out position. You can have them touch the toe on the knee, then the ankle and then down onto the floor as in a contemporary dance class.

3. From this balance position, ask the dancers what would they need to do to fall forwards or sideways or backwards. They can experiment to see if they need to rise on one foot, tip the torso in a tilt, extend the leg in retiré, drop the head, perform an arm gesture or try to turn. You could add more to this list. Dancers may land from the balance in a lunge, run, onto the floor on a low level or into

another balance on the other leg. Prompt them to try both legs and all combinations of the falling action and reaction.

4. Set the combination that the dancers will try and ask them to remember each movement as they go so that they can create a phrase. Here are some possible combinations:

    a. Retiré in parallel with the right leg, rise to fall and land in a lunge to the side.

    b. Retiré in turnout with the left leg, swing both the body and an arm to the left to fall into the floor. Then recover and retiré with the right foot in parallel, drop the head forwards into a run and add an arm line.

5. After giving three set combinations to get the dancers moving, ask them to add on two that they thought really worked for them from their original improvisation.

6. Ask the dancers to perform this sequence as a whole, keeping it going until the end so that the movements seem to logically join together. If they don't seem to fit logically, have dancers edit their movements to fit.

7. Have pairs of dancers watch each other's work. Ask them to advise their partners on how to tease out the high points. Advice could be simply inhaling before the fall at the point of suspension, making movements bigger or adding jumps.

8. To get your dancers thinking spontaneously, have them work in pairs and perform their sequence to an audience. This time, when one is up or in retiré, just before the fall the other is at a low level or just recovering from the fall. Ask the dancers observing to discuss what was effective about this.

Teaching Tip

You can use this improvisation again, but instead of falling from retiré dancers could find alternative positions (e.g., arabesque, attitude, a rise, a freeze or other shapes in which dancers balance on one leg). You can suggest these positions or have dancers come up with their own.

Further Development

The dancers can set some of the movements in the duets and find moments where they could push their partner to the floor or have a counterbalance with another dancer before they fall off balance. It is possible to find moments to give and take weight or even lift a partner once.

Rhythm Do

This improvisation gets dancers to think about the sounds that they make when they are dancing, how they can create rhythms with their bodies and how they can use this concept in performance. It is useful to have done Sign In (page 70) or Body Part Conversation (page 106) before this task. Have dancers warm up with a warm-up game or technical exercises.

1. Ask the dancers to stand away from other dancers and create a rhythm. It may even be from a song they know. You can have them first clap it, then walk or stamp it until they have created something they like.

2. Next, have dancers try to perform the rhythm using different body parts. Ask them to move around the room with the rhythm in their bodies. Dancers may find it helpful to have some movements that are sounds from steps or one body part making con-

A dancer uses both hands to click out a rhythm.

tact with another, stamping, slapping and clicking. They should come up with ideas they feel confident about.

3. Ask them to play with the rhythm (e.g., by travelling, jumping and turning) and to loop the sequence together so that they can repeat the phrase.

4. Have the dancers work in pairs and show each other their movements (or, if they struggle to remember the rhythm and movements, the basic improvisation idea).

5. Have dancers use each other's rhythm to create another phrase added on to their own. They could also include sounds by making contact with each other. So, they will have their own phrase and possibly a new phrase with the same rhythm as their partner.

6. Next, use the element of chance to get them to go where they like in the space and interact with whomever they want but still keeping their own rhythm going. This could be half the group doing and half the group watching.

7. You can create a whole group improvisation in which dancers add on to their own rhythmic phrase as you build the improvisation. You may need to have some basic rules so the dancers can choose or know the following:

- When to come into the space
- When to stop
- When to either lie, sit or kneel
- When to walk in circles
- When to travel backwards
- When to travel on straight and curved pathways
- When to leave the space

Teaching Tip

Try having the audience half of the group play instruments or make percussion sounds to accompany the dancers.

Further Development

The dancers can set some of the movements that they came up with in the duets. If you have recorded the improvisation on video, the group can watch it and discuss which moments worked, then perhaps re-create them in a group composition.

Forty-Five Degrees

This is an improvisation for dancers to try on their own; they will be exploring the movements that their own bodies can do. They will need to be warmed up so that they are ready to create.

1. Ask the dancers to find a space in the dance studio with any facing and then explore the movement that both arms can do if they only move 45 degrees in any plane. Tell them to create movements that are unlike anyone else's in the room. They can lead the movement with the elbow. It may be that the arms make angles together or in the air or around the body. Ask the dancers to remember five movements that they have selected from

A dancer investigates angles made with her whole body.

their improvisations and combine them together to make a short motif. Have them try the exercise again with an angle of a different size; 90 degrees works well.

2. Using the same idea of the angle, ask the dancers to explore the same idea with the legs. They may use kicks and gestures as well as steps and turns that take the angles into account. Ask the dancers again to select about five movements to create another motif. For example, they may step forward, swing a leg, step back into a lunge, turn, jump and retiré.

3. Ask the dancers to face a preselected partner or anyone near to them in the space and show their arm and leg sequence. Have them give each other feedback based on two key observations, such as use of levels or where they are focusing with their eyes and how this can help the dance.

4. Have dancers put the arm and leg phrases together using these possibilities:

- ◎ **Unison:** The arms and legs work together at the same time.
- ◎ **Canon:** The leg gestures and arm gestures happen one after another; this could be both legs and then both arms or one leg one arm keep moving.
- ◎ **Adding:** Put new arm gestures together with the original leg sequence and use the bottom half of the body with the arm sequence.

5. Have dancers share their work and give feedback in slightly bigger groups. They can discuss whether it was effective, what worked and what they would do differently if they did it again.

Teaching Tip

If they struggle to come up with movements on their own, dancers could work in pairs and either push and pull each other at 45 degrees or suggest to each other what part can move where.

Further Development

Dancers can develop these ideas into sequences and try performing them to different pieces of music. If some movement material stands out, dancers can teach it to the rest of the group and create a small group or whole group piece.

Encounters

This improvisation works well to get dancers to be aware of each other, prepare them to interact and perhaps create contact moments. It raises awareness of the use of space and travelling by creating shapes or tableau for other dancers to go under, over, through, on, past and around. Dancers are forced to make movement choices. Before doing this improvisation, dancers need to be warmed up with a warm-up game or technical exercises. You can have them do Introduce the Space (page 56) to prepare them for this improvisation.

Dancers make shapes for the other half of the group to encounter.

1. Ask the dancers to walk around the room considering the floor plan or pathway that they are creating as they travel. If they create a pathway that they can remember and repeat, this may make the next task more interesting. Ask the dancers to freeze on your command. Whilst they are pausing, give each dancer a number 1 or 2 and ask them to walk again. You can challenge the group to find their own way of travelling around the space.

2. Let them know that you want the number 1's to keep travelling and the number 2's to create still obstacles, or shapes that block the travellers' paths when you give a signal (it could be "Freeze"). The shapes or statues can use any level, as long as they are interesting. After the signal, advise the travellers that if they have a dancer

blocking their pathway, they must not avoid them but rather get past them in interesting ways (go over, under, on or through them). You may need to demonstrate or pick a dancer to repeat an action that you thought worked.

3. Ask the dancers to switch roles. If you think it is creating interesting work, you can have them switch again and repeat.

4. Next, ask the dancers to get into groups of five or six and number themselves. The aim of the number that you will call out (make sure all have been called at some point) is to travel around the space. One dancer in each group travels. The other four or five dancers are to block the pathway of that dancer with different shapes created at different levels along the pathway. These may be in a line. Again, encourage dancers to find interesting ways to get past each other. As the dancer finds a way past a shape, that dancer can then move to create a new shape at the end of the other numbers. You can try calling two numbers at the same time so that two dancers are trying to pass three or four shapes.

5. If the dancers are working well it is possible to do this with the whole group making a group tableau, one after another in front of one travelling dancer.

Teaching Tip

Make sure that the dancers are not using the same movement response every time that they encounter another dancer. Try suggesting some new ideas or showing what other dancers are doing. You could point out movements that you don't want to see again.

Further Development

This improvisation can lead to creating group dance pieces and using a tableau in one section. You could also ask the dancers to re-create all the actions that they performed when interacting and passing the obstacles with the same dynamic and timing, but without the other dancers in the space.

CHAPTER 5

EXPLORING CONTACT IMPROVISATION

The improvisations in this chapter introduce dancers to contact improvisation. You can use them to develop dancers' awareness of each other and their sense of trust whilst still being responsible for themselves. Exploring movement through contact improvisation helps dancers develop confidence, too. It is important to note that dancers have different levels of understanding and sophistication; one dancer may freely give his or her weight, and another may not want to be touched and find lifts a real challenge. The whole concept of making a connection with touching, lifting or taking the weight of another dancer's body can have very different demands on dancers both physically and emotionally. Therefore some exercises in this chapter explore the idea of touch before dancers need to give and take weight. Dancers will need a level of maturity to begin to develop their trust levels as well as their confidence with these improvisations. If an improvisation does not work, this could be for any reason from all the dancers not listening to taking it seriously or missing key commands. Don't worry; they may not be ready for this type of activity yet. You may want to try Keep the Awareness (page 143) and Palms (page 128) before Offer a Platform (page 130) and Counterbalance (page 134). When choosing improvisations involving lifts, keep in mind that some dancers like to try individual lifts (such as in Find Five Lifts, page 137) before being open to the give and take of manipulation activities (such as in Lava Lamp, page 122). Whatever the level of your dancers' maturity or skill, the improvisations in this chapter help them explore ways to successfully shift weight through space and react to other bodies, objects and varying forces.

The Connection

This improvisation explores the idea of making and maintaining body part connections with other dancers and exploring movement possibilities. It develops trust between members of the group and their awareness of each other and what choices they make from one moment to the next. It is a good initial improvisation to introduce contact work and can act as a gauge to see how mature the group's approach is to this type of more intimate movement creation. Before doing this task, have dancers warm up with a warm-up game or technical exercises.

1. Ask the dancers to find a partner and hold hands.

2. Ask them to explore how they can travel around the room together. As they walk, run, pull and turn, have them find ways to go under or over each other and perhaps use counterbalances or moments of weight taking. Remind them to be aware of the other pairs of dancers in the room.

3. Ask the dancers to quickly find a new partner and make a connection with the head, creating head-to-head contact. They must be careful not to knock heads, so they must maintain the contact as they move. Ask them to try gently pushing their partner with the head and exploring how they can travel, especially trying different

Dancers explore movement possibilities with their heads connected.

levels. At this point you can also have them try foot-to-foot or elbow-to-elbow contact.

4. Ask the dancers to find a new partner and this time to each have a different body part in contact with their partner (e.g., head-to-knee or elbow-to-shoulder contact). You can set the first body part, then ask the dancers to come up with different combinations themselves.

5. If step 4 is successful, try a more complex approach: Have dancers call out two body parts themselves and when both are said, they can quickly find a partner and connect their two parts, then continue to travel together.

6. Ask the dancers in their pairs to create a short sequence or phrase that uses these connections. They can swap and have different body parts connecting as they dance, but what ever happens, they must have some contact between them throughout.

7. Encourage dancers to avoid using their hands as contact points and to find new ways of working.

8. Have dancers share their work in groups of two or three pairs at a time.

Teaching Tip

You can walk around the space, giving pairs feedback. Try using music to create a dynamic, classical or rhythmic response.

Further Development

The dancers can set some of the movements that they come up with in the duets and start to phrase the material, thinking about where the high points are in the performance. Some duets that might not have used lifts or counterbalances could see where there are moments that this could naturally occur. The dancers could explore how different choreographic devices can change the movement material.

Lava Lamp

This is an improvisation for pairs of dancers. It requires dancers to respond to moments that could happen in contact improvisation. It can be developed from Energy Impulses (page 78). It involves touch, so be sure it is appropriate for your group.

1. Ask the dancers to find a partner and a space in the room away from other dancers.

2. Explain that one dancer is the energy and one is a lava lamp that will rise and fall. This visual idea may give the dancer an under-standable dynamic to use. The energy dancer stands behind the partner and plays with moving the shoulders. For example, the dancer could place both hands on each shoulder and push and pull the shoulders to make them go up and down and rotate, either both together or in different directions. This movement must be very gentle and slow at first so that the lava lamp can respond. The lava lamp dancer must let the body be moved and move with the flow of the energy given.

Dancers manipulate a partner's shoulders. Dancers start slowly so the lava lamp can respond.

3. Next, have the energy dancer do the same thing with the hips, again gentle at first so that the lava lamp's responses are true to the force being used.

4. Now have them start to use both the shoulders and the hips at the same time, keeping the movements fluid like the liquid in a lava lamp.

5. Have the dancers swap roles and try the exercise again.

6. If the dancers are working well they can start to introduce different body parts and try to move their partners around the room.

7. If this is working well, both dancers can try to be both the energy and the lava lamp and have a go at improvising together, coming back together and letting their weight help them to move. In this case, both dancers manipulate and respond to manipulations; there may be moments of contact, counterbalance or even lifts.

Teaching Tip

The lava lamp dancer may respond better with the eyes closed.

Further Development

Use this improvisation with Clay Sculpting (page 124). The dancers could respond to the energy being given to take them into new movements. They could use this way of moving to put transitions into Find Five Lifts (page 137).

Clay Sculpting

This is a trust-based task that you can use as an introduction to contact improvisation. It asks dancers to remember what it felt like to be moved in terms of force, timing, correct use of space and quality. It can also get dancers thinking about how they can create original movement material.

1. Have dancers work with a partner. If groups are uneven, they can work in groups of three; two dancers can play the same role or they can each take turns as a third observer.

2. Ask the dancers to face each other and decide who is sculptor and who is the clay. They will switch roles later.

3. Ask the sculptor to gently move the partner's body parts to mould the clay into an artistic shape. For example, they can make fingers point or manipulate the face to create facial expressions. Some common answers include the teapot position or a finger up the nose. Although you may find these answers obvious or crude, remember that the dancers are being creative.

Dancers create positions with their partners.

4. Ask the dancers to create five more interesting sculptures. Repeating the exercise helps them get used to working this way.

5. Have dancers switch roles and repeat the exercise as many times as they did it the first time.

6. Next, have the sculptor use five steps to manipulate the clay into a shape or position; the clay dancer must remember each step and then perform it again as if the sculptor is moving them. The final position is not as important as remembering and performing how the dancer got there. This often creates a wonderful quality of move-

ment, but some dancers do it better with their eyes closed because it can be easier to recall how a movement *felt* in the body.

7. Have dancers try the task several times, switching roles each time and focusing on recalling the movements with the same force, timing, use of space and quality.

8. Ask dancers to perform their movements for each other with the eyes closed then with eyes open. Ask them if they see a difference in the movements.

9. Dancers will end up with short motifs that can be shared with others.

Teaching Tip

The dancers could do this without touching and instead call out which body parts they want to move and where they want it to go. They could also give the movements a speed or dynamic (e.g., "Move your left arm in a circle to the floor, starting and stopping as you go").

Further Development

Dancers can learn each other's phrase or indeed start again with a partner and create a longer phrase of movement this time with considered force and use of timing.

Circle of Trust

This is a whole group trust exercise that can often be difficult for some members. It gives you a good idea about who may be able to cope with contact work and who finds it a challenge. It can give confidence to dancers that have not given their weight before.

1. Ask the dancers to form a large circle in the space. To ensure that dancers are evenly spaced, ask them to be the same distance from the dancer on their right as from the dancer on their left. Have dancers stand shoulder to shoulder; they need to be as close as possible to be a support for each other. If the group is large and the circle is too big to safely catch a falling dancer, split it into several smaller circles.

2. Have one dancer stand in the centre of the circle with the eyes closed; the other dancers close the circle tightly and put their arms up in front to prepare to catch.

3. Ask the dancer in the centre to lean back with the legs straight; if keeping the body straight is difficult, the knees may bend.

One dancer falls off balance to be caught by the whole group.

4. The dancers behind the falling dancer must accept his or her weight with their hands and push the dancer gently back to the centre.

5. Have the dancer repeat the lean in any direction; each time he or she is gently pushed back to the centre.

6. Ask another dancer to enter the circle and repeat the exercise until all dancers have tried it.

7. If you have a large group, you can split up the circle into several smaller circles. If this is the case, either make sure that each group fully understands the exercise before trying it, or ask the groups to take it in turns so that you and the groups can observe each circle.

8. When the dancers feel confident with giving and taking weight, they can start to use different body parts to catch the central dancer with. For example, one dancer could offer a leg or a back for the dancer to lean on.

9. If the exercise is working well and enough trust has been developed, try leading into counterbalances and even lifts. Hands could pull and the centre dancer could fall onto another dancer's back or side.

Teaching Tip

You can have dancers develop the quality and force of their catching movements, but ask them to be gentle at first; because this is a trust exercise, their primary purpose is not to let the centre dancer fall.

Further Development

This improvisation could lead into Offer a Platform (page 130). You may want to develop this task over time and repeat it so that the dancers can work on their own confidence with trusting others to not let them fall. Dancers also need to develop the skills to catch themselves if indeed they are not caught. The dancer in the circle can start to be more active and push away from other dancers.

Palms

This improvisation is for pairs of dancers and could be a further development from Clay Sculpting (page 124). During this task, dancers gain experience responding to moments in contact improvisation. It involves giving some weight, so be sure it is appropriate for your group.

1. Ask the dancers to find a partner and a space in the room away from other dancers.

2. Have the dancers face each other and extend their arms forward; one dancer has palms up and the other has palms down. The dancer with palms down puts both hands on top of the partner's hands.

3. Have the palms-down partner close the eyes and give the full weight of the hands and arms to the other dancer. Tell the palms-up dancer to take the partner's weight and then begin to slowly move their arms, perhaps in a circle on every plane.

Dancers give the weight of the arm to a partner through the hands.

4. Next, have dancers switch roles and try it again.

5. If the dancers are working well together, have them introduce more ideas, such as moving in different directions and manipulating or even dropping and catching their partner's arms.

6. Have both dancers try the exercise again using other body parts and once they have gained trust, they can explore with their eyes open. If they can give their weight with their eyes open, they will be able to watch the movement that they are creating whilst hopefully authentically responding to their partner.

Teaching Tip

Start small and simple at first to develop the ideas of giving weight; it takes some dancers longer than others to develop this level of trust.

Further Development

This exercise could lead to Keep the Awareness (page 143). Giving dancers an idea of the weight of another dancer is key in understanding how to make weight in contact work. Try having dancers work in pairs; dancer A lies on the floor whilst dancer B weighs each of dancer A's body parts. For example, dancer B can pick up an arm and feel how heavy it is, then pick up a leg and so on. When replacing body parts on the floor, dancer B must do so gently. Also caution dancers about safely lifting the head. Often dancers are surprised by the weight of the head. Dancer B must gently place both hands under the neck and slide it under the head; dancer A must stay relaxed and not lift the head. For optimal control, kneeling near the crown of the head works best. Have dancers switch roles and try the exercise again.

Offer a Platform

This trust-based task can function as an introduction into lifts in contact improvisation. Dancers act as a body platform and give their weight to a partner, so they must be responsible for their safety.

Dancers give weight to backs and legs.

1. Have dancers work with a partner. If groups are uneven, they can work in groups of three; two dancers can play the same role or they can each take turns as a third observer.

2. Have one dancer get down on all fours to make a platform. The other dancer lies across the platform without touching the floor, giving the body's weight to the platform. Have this dancer try to roll off the platform forwards or backwards. The idea is to explore ways to get on and off the platform.

3. Next, have dancers try different balances on the platform different ways to get on and off.

4. Have dancers switch roles and try the exercise again.

5. Next, have the dancers try this exercise with a living platform: As the dancer rolls or slides off the platform, the platform begins to roll, too, and tries not to lose contact. The dancers keep rolling until they have switched roles; the dancer on top has now become the platform. Have them repeat the exercise.

6. Next, have one partner offer a new support: The platform stands in a second position plié; the feet naturally turn out about 1 metre apart with the knees bent. The supporting dancer can use the arms to help the other dancer into lifts or hold him or her in a position. To avoid lifting with the lower back, the support must not lean forwards. The support could even try travelling. Have the dancer explore where to lean or hold on to the platform in order to come off the floor. Examples include arms around the waist, climbing up on the thighs and placing a foot at the top of the thigh.

7. Have the dancers switch roles and try step 6 again.

8. If dancers are working successfully together, have them try body surfing: One dancer lies on the floor and the other dancer gives weight by lying in any direction on top of the platform. To do this well, the dancer must relax and totally let go of any tension. Dancers must just be aware of their partner's joints. The platform partner must find the easiest way to roll or move.

9. Have dancers switch roles and try step 8 again. Have them further explore what works and also to discuss what happens if they lie in different places on the body.

10. If you have time remaining, you can have the group use these platforms in a short improvisation. The dancers need to walk around the whole space then find one person to follow, stepping in their rhythm close behind them until centres are connected, back and front. One dancer rolls down through the spine to all fours and the other partner makes and keeps contact. Finally, dancers find a way to roll off and up to standing position to find another partner.

Teaching Tip

Encourage dancers to explore new types of platforms. For safety, have one pair stand near another pair as they experiment.

Further Development

This exercise could develop into Find Five Lifts (page 137). You may also use it before Lava Lamp (page 122). Include platforms as a way of moving from moment to moment.

Two Against One

This improvisation is for three dancers. It is a fun way to demonstrate the ease of movement necessary for contact improvisation. As with many of the improvisations in this section, maturity is needed by the dancers, especially for the latter part of this improvisation. For this improvisation, dancers will need to have experienced previous improvisations such as Introduce the Space (page 56) so that this is not the first contact improvisation used or the first time that they used their weight.

Dancers try both tasks in the improvisation.

1. Ask the dancers to find two other dancers to make a trio and find a space in the room away from other dancers.

2. Have two of the dancers cross their arms and offer this position as a seat to support the third dancer under the legs.

3. The supported dancer sits on the arms and places his or her own arms around the necks of the two other dancers. The supported dancer must try to get to the floor and the other two dancers must try to stop him or her.

4. Remind the dancers that the two lifters can use muscle strength but the supported dancer needs to release tension. Dancers may struggle at first; tell them that it helps to imagine oneself as water. Ask, "How quickly can you get to the floor?"

5. Ask the dancers to switch roles until they all have a chance to explore being lifted and trying to get to the floor.

6. Give the dancers an opportunity to discuss what happened.

7. Next, have one dancer lie on the floor and the other two sit or lie on top. The dancer on the floor must try to stand up. You may want to make this a timed exercise so that if dancers are struggling, they don't get trapped for too long.

8. The two dancers on top must use their strength to keep the dancer on the floor.

9. You may let the dancers struggle before this approach: Advise the dancer on the floor to take the path of least resistance; think "Up," be relaxed and possibly roll to get up from the floor. It is possible.

10. Again, give the dancers the chance to swap roles and discuss what happened.

Teaching Tip

This task is about having the right quality of movements. If one group seems to understand this concept, have that group demonstrate the movements to the others.

Further Development

You can combine this exercise with Find Five Lifts (page 137), using three dancers instead of two. You may want to try the task again, this time giving more description to the dancers to help them understand how sometimes not fighting the forces that can act on them can also produce the same results. Use words such as *liquid, fluid* and *relax.*

Counterbalance

This improvisation asks dancers to give and take weight through several parts of the body. To help avoid injuries from slipping, have dancers work in bare feet or wear training shoes. Also, explain your instructions carefully to avoid misunderstandings that lead to injury.

1. Have dancers work with a partner. If groups are uneven, they can work in groups of three; two dancers can play the same role or they can each take turns as a third observer.

2. Ask the dancers to sit back to back with the knees up (they could do the first part of Body Part Conversation, page 106) and try to stand up together. They may be able to do this easily; a more challenging test is when you tell them to press their backs together whilst standing, bend their knees and return to the floor. Dancers should use the force of their backs pressing together, not rely on their leg strength, to complete this movement.

Dancers give weight back to back.

3. Have the dancers switch partners and repeat the exercise many times. Changing partners encourages dancers to feel different body weights and focus on the action of pressing the backs together. When dancers do not use that force, the exercise becomes more difficult. If one partner keeps slipping, have that dancer put the feet against a wall.

4. Next, have dancers face each other, hold the same one of each other's hands (right hand to right or left hand to left) and repeat the action of bending to the floor and returning upwards. This time, the force must come from holding whilst leaning back and pulling rather than from pressing. Both dancers' arms need to be fully extended before they embark on bending the knees. If this grip is not secure enough, have dancers hold wrists. You may have dancers try holding both hands first before using just one. It is helpful for dancers to position the feet in parallel and close to each other.

Dancers pull up from the floor.

5. Again, have dancers repeat the exercise with as many other dancers in the group as possible.

6. Next, have dancers try a variation: They let go of each other's hand and switch to holding the other hand whilst leaning back. So, dancers go down bending their knees and come up to standing, then suddenly swap hands and catch each other quickly before they go down to the floor again.

7. Using this grip and counterbalance, try these variations:

   a. One dancer remains standing whilst the partner bends to the floor and comes back up. Then they switch roles.

   b. One dancer bends the knees and lowers to the floor whilst the partner rolls down through the spine until they are both lying down with their knees up. If the partner runs backwards in the roll-down position, he or she can then pull the other dancer off the floor into a jump or maybe even into a lift.

   c. Whilst one dancer is down the pair can make contact with the lower back on the floor. The standing partner can pull his or her arm backwards to make partner on the floor spin on the back. To spin fast, the dancer on the floor must lie on the lower back. The standing dancer needs to change the grip or let go so as not to twist the other dancer's arm.

8. Ask the dancers to find a final partner and explore other body parts that can pull or push against each other to create a balance. They can try shoulder to shoulder, either facing each other or side by side or stepping out from each other to see if they can still balance. Other ideas to try are shoulder to hips, hand to shoulder and hands to hips. Ask the dancers to find two more body part combinations and then share their movements with the other dancers.

9. At this point you can have dancers create a short demonstration of each of the exciting moments that they came up with in pairs.

Teaching Tip

There is quite a lot to cover here; you may need to build it up over a number of sessions.

Further Development

This exercise could lead to Offer a Platform (page 130); even if you have tried it before, this time you may get more open responses. Or, each of the moments could be used in a structured improvisation where dancers meet each other, perform an action and then find another partner.

Find Five Lifts

This improvisation asks dancers to give and take weight. Carefully explain and observe the giving and taking of weight to minimise chances of injury. Dancers may want to do Offer a Platform (page 130) to warm up and prepare for this improvisation.

Lifting a dancer upside down.

A dancer takes the weight on her legs.

Lifting a dancer on the hips.

Lifting a dancer straight and upside down.

1. Have dancers work with a partner. If groups are uneven, they can work in groups of three; two dancers can play the same role or they can each take turns as a third observer. Or, you could do this improvisation as a trio.

2. Ask the dancers to work together and find five different ways of lifting each other. You may give them some ideas to try first. You can give dancers several minutes to find each lift, then clearly name them from number 1 to number 5.

3. Have dancers show the rest of the group each of their lifts and invite them to comment about how they can be enhanced with arm or leg gestures. Ask the audience to think about what the lift may mean: Is it a fight, a relationship, an object being lifted or worn?

4. Ask the dancers to find ways into and out of each lift to give a continuous feel to this short duet. They may notice movement material that they can use in choreography or they could explore the notion of manipulating each other that they may have experienced in Lava Lamp (page 122).

Teaching Tip

You may need to explain to the dancers the difference between lifting a dancer using your brute strength and lifting using your skeletal frame. Leaning forward to lift can injure the lower back. The hip or shoulders are good skeletal places to help with a lift because they require using less muscle power.

Further Development

Have dancers create a contact duet per pair that they can use as part of a duet or a bigger piece. Dancers could pair up with another couple to learn each other's duets or you could collect all the best moments from every duet and teach them to the whole group. Dancers can work in groups of four to play with unison and canon or even try Taking Away (see page 157).

Crowd Surfing

This improvisation is a whole group trust exercise. It can be difficult for some dancers; after trying it, you will have a very good idea about which dancers are able to cope with contact work. It can give confidence to dancers that have not given their weight before. You can develop this task from Circle of Trust (page 126).

1. Have one dancer lie on the floor and the rest of the group lift them up very slowly. This may take several attempts and will need everyone to join in.

2. Have the dancers try this: One dancer is lifted above the heads of the other dancers and stays here while the dancers below move in one direction, peeling themselves from one end and rejoining at another end.

3. The supporters can take the dancer down again towards the floor, allowing the movement to feel organic and fluid.

4. Once the group below is happy with what they are doing, the supported dancer can stretch, roll, relax, dive and fully explore being lifted in all directions.

5. Get the group to place the dancer on the floor and step away.

6. Have dancers try this exercise again with a different supported dancer until all dancers have had a chance to be lifted.

Many dancers keep one dancer up high.

7. Once the dancers feel confident with this exercise, try having one dancer run into the group with the arms outstretched, ready to be lifted.

Teaching Tip

Try this task with the smallest member of the group first so that everyone can see that it is possible and understand where they need to be.

Further Development

This task of being lifted up high develops confidence but with the buffer of many hands. You could try it again with smaller groups. The aim is to be lifted high just by one other dancer. You may want to try it on a very soft surface, perhaps with gym mats.

Falling

This improvisation asks the dancers to give and take weight. Remember to carefully explain the giving and taking of weight to minimise chances of injuries. Dancers may want to do Offer a Platform (page 130) to prepare for this improvisation.

1. Have dancers work with a partner. If groups are uneven, they can work in groups of three; they can each take turns as a third observer.

2. Ask one dancer to stand behind the other and have both face the same direction. The dancer behind places the hands just below the partner's shoulder blades. The front dancer leans back and gives his or her weight to the partner. This action is easier if the supported dancer bends at the knees instead of the waist to form a straight line from the head to the knees.

3. Have the supporter gently push the other dancer back to standing. The leaning dancer can build from small movements to perhaps leaning on the hands, back and leg of the support. When they feel confident, the duo can play with falling and catching.

Dancers fall backwards and give their weight and trust to a partner.

4. Ask the dancers to switch roles and try the exercise again.

5. You can have the dancer fall in different directions—sideways, forwards or even turning before falling, turning as they fall, catching and guiding to the floor.

6. You can have dancers try this task again in threes with two supporters, or even one falling, one supporting and one pulling. Another option is to try catching the dancer with both arms under the armpits. From here the lifter could tip them onto one side so that they step the leg over into a lunge.

7. If time allows and dancers are able, have them perform duets for each other and comment on their work.

Teaching Tip

The dancers could catch their partner after they have just tipped off balance and, as they grow in confidence, allow the partner to fall and be caught closer to the floor.

Further Development

Dancers can work in pairs to create a simple contact phrase to use as part of a duet or a bigger piece. Pairs of dancers could work together in groups of four to learn each other's duets, or you could select all the best moments from every duet and teach them to the whole group.

Keep the Awareness

This improvisation focuses on the idea of making and maintaining body part connections with other dancers and exploring movement possibilities. It develops trust between dancers and raises their awareness of each other's movements from one moment to the next. Before doing this improvisation, have dancers warm up with a warm-up task or technical exercises. You can have dancers try The Connection (page 120) to prepare for this exercise.

1. Ask the dancers to find a partner. They will travel across the room together from a given point to another.

2. Have one dancer use a body part to lead their journey across the floor.

3. Remind dancers to create an interesting pathway whilst using all levels and varying the momentum. Suggest creative ways to lead the movement, such as leading with the head.

4. Have the other dancer place a hand on his or her partner's head and keep it there the whole time that they travel across the room. At this stage, the partner must not respond to the hand. This is so that the second dancer can keep contact whilst another dances.

Two dancers make simple connections.

5. Have dancers switch roles and experience the exercise again.

6. Next, change the body part that leads the movement and which body part they use to keep the connection.

7. Now, try the exercise again; this time the dancer responds to the hand (or other body part) by pushing it away or pulling it to get a response from the partner.

8. Have dancers continue, naturally reversing roles as they respond to each other. They can change leading and touching body parts and take it to different levels and directions.

Teaching Tip

To build trust and develop dancers' skills, try introducing each stage of this exercise over several sessions.

Further Development

Have dancers take the movements they created and phrase them, thinking about where the high points are.

Jelly Bubble

This improvisation is for three dancers. It is a fun way to demonstrate the ease of movement necessary for contact improvisation.

1. Ask the dancers to find two other dancers to make a trio and find a space in the room away from other dancers.

2. Jelly: Tell one dancer to imagine that his or her body has no bones or that the body is jelly jointed; the other two dancers must try to keep the dancer upright. They can lift, carry or manipulate, but the jelly dancer must give his or her weight totally to the other two dancers.

3. Ask the dancers to switch roles and try the exercise again until they all have a chance to explore being lifted and manipulated.

4. Give the dancers an opportunity to discuss what happened.

5. Bubble: Next, ask one of the dancers to imagine that he or she is a bubble and perhaps go in between the other two dancers.

6. The other two dancers try to push, pull or lift the bubble in different directions. The bubble dancer should feel like a big floating ball that is slow and purposeful; remind the dancer to release all tension in his or her movements.

7. Ask the dancers to switch roles and try the exercise again until they all have a chance to explore being lifted and manipulated.

One dancer as jelly with two supporting dancers.

8. Ask the trios to come up with one more idea that is similar to a jelly or a bubble and encourage them to use a very different dynamic. If they struggle with this idea, suggest simple elements such as fire, air or water.

Teaching Tip

If certain dancers are working well together, have them show their work to the rest of the group and discuss what worked.

Further Development

You could convert this exercise into Find Five Lifts (page 137) with three dancers instead of two.

DEVELOPING IMPROVISATIONS

This chapter provides ways to develop the movement material created using chapters 2 through 5. Once you and your dancers have made motifs, phrases or sequences, you can use the suggestions in this chapter to manipulate, develop and adapt the movement material. Most of the tasks in this chapter can also work with a phrase taught in technique class, a sequence learnt from a professional company's repertoire or a sequence created from one of the improvisations in this book. It is helpful for the dancers to learn the phrases to be used before doing each development.

Parts, Not the Whole

This improvisation uses a whole phrase that all the dancers know; the task challenges how well they know it. The phrase is fragmented and different dancers use different parts of it, so you must clarify the actions, timing and location of each moment in the movement material.

Dancers use arm actions only.

1. Ask the dancers to get into small groups and remind themselves of the movement material and to really understand the intricacies and timing of the phrase.

2. Split the whole group into four groups for the next stage.

3. Ask one group to focus on going over the footwork but to change what is happening in the top half of the body. In other words, they perform the same steps and actions into and out of the floor but the torso, head and arms need to be different from the original.

4. Ask another group to use the original movements for the upper body with arm gestures and maybe the torso, but change what the lower body performs. This could involve being still or adding steps or jumps or even turns that could have the same rhythm as the original or be very different.

5. Ask one group to create a new sequence using the same rhythmic pattern as the original. If dancers struggle with this task, this could have some of the same movement material somewhere in the sequence. Encourage questions from the dancers about what they want to do; asking questions means they are thinking about possibilities.

6. Ask one group to take the original idea behind the movement or the main features or aspect that they like from the sequence (e.g., the use of turns, long lines, contractions) and to create new movement that is based on this idea.

7. Ask each group to perform their development so that everyone can see different possibilities for developing the original material.

Teaching Tip

If you ask younger groups to work independently on this task, you may need to give them some input and encouragement to push a diverse outcome.

Further Development

You will end up with four new sequences that can then be used in a group piece to show the development of ideas.

RADS and Restrictions

Use a known sequence so that the possible developments have clarity. This development uses the RADS (relationships, actions, dynamics and use of space) to give the movement material a restriction therefore turning it into something different. This is a good experimental development as there are lots of suggested ideas to explore.

Relationships

1. Have dancers work in pairs. One dancer performs the sequence whilst another tries to stop them by holding onto a body part. This could also be two dancers moving and one stopping or one dancer moving and two restricting.

One dancer with a hand on her head as a restriction.

2. One dancer needs to get in the way of the one performing at different levels so the dancer has to dance over, under or around the partner.

3. One dancer performs the phrase whilst the other tries to give weight to him or her in some way.

4. One dancer performs whilst the other one tries to lift, support and move him or her to a different space.

Actions

1. Have dancers try to perform the phrase using only extended arms and legs to make the movements.

2. Ask dancers to try the phrase with a constant falling action, as if the dancer is falling through the air.

3. Have them try to dance the sequence with both arms and legs crossed.

Dynamics

1. Ask dancers to perform the sequence with the legs very heavy and the torso and arms trying to move them to keep up.
2. Have dancers perform the sequence as fast as possible within 5 seconds.

Space

1. Ask dancers to perform the sequence in a limited space (e.g., 15 cm by 15 cm). The dancer could also be stuck in some way to the floor.
2. Have them perform the whole sequence lying on the floor.
3. Have them perform the sequence at a low level, perhaps with a partner, making sure that the dancer does not go above a certain height.
4. Have each dancer perform the sequence on a floor plan designed by another dancer.

Teaching Tip

Do not try all RADS possibilities in one lesson; you can even use one per lesson or repeat one over and over again.

Further Development

Dancers can create a new phrase from each possibility and put them together to make a section of choreography using any chance methods.

Zoo Line

This improvisation can work with any sequence created from one of the improvisations in this book. It works best when dancers each have their own movement phrase. If the dancers use the same sequence, they need to start at a different place in the sequence so that they are not simultaneously doing the same movement as the person next to them.

1. Ask the dancers to go over the phrase and to make it stationary at a fixed point. They can lunge and drop to the floor, but always come back to the spot that they are dancing on.

2. Ask the dancers to get into a line, shoulder to shoulder and facing the front. This could be as a whole group or in smaller groups of five or six. The closer the dancers are, the better for making contact.

3. Tell each dancer to perform the sequence with an awareness of the adjacent person so that everyone moves at the same time. Movement may slow down at first to avoid collisions. Dancers should pay attention to see if any great moments happen by chance.

Dancers in a line work together.

4. Next, have the dancer at the end of the line work with the adjacent dancer and relate to that dancer in some way. Have them try complementing, contrasting, pushing, pulling, nudging, supporting and any other movements that present themselves. Have the dancers in the middle do the same thing but with the dancers on each side of

them. The dancers can start moving slowly to let partners know what they are doing and to explore what they can do to relate to them.

5. Each dancer must relate to the other dancers on both sides at the same time. Dancers can start to all do this together if they are working well as a group.

6. Have all the dancers perform their sequences together, perhaps with slight adaptation so that it creates opportunities for interesting moments.

7. Have groups show each other their work and share ideas. They may also join together to make one long line.

Teaching Tip

Having the dancers face a mirror can really help the whole line see what is happening.

Further Development

This zoo line works well in a piece of choreography where the dancers come together for the line, perform and then move away one at a time. It works well at the back or front of a stage, especially with a large group of dancers who spread across the width of the stage.

Fill the Space

The dancers need to use a movement phrase or sequence that they have created or learnt. This development looks at the space between dancers. Dancers explore personal space and, depending on age and experience, perhaps even contact, support or counterbalance.

1. Have dancers work in pairs. Have one dancer perform the phrase and the other dancer observe; where it moves and what actions are performed.

2. Have the first dancer repeat the phrase. Whilst the first dancer moves, the other dancer improvises movements to fill the space around the first dancer. These new movements could include moments from the initial phrase if both dancers know it or some completely new complementary movement.

Two dancers closely relate to each other spatially.

3. Have dancers explore further. They can create relationships using touch, manipulation, support, contrast and complement.

4. If desired, have the dancers switch roles and repeat the exercise to create a longer duet.

Teaching Tip

The dancers may try the phrase once at full speed to see what interesting movements or moments are created, but the dancer improvising may not be able to keep up. In that case, get the dancers to create it in steps; perform one movement and the response movement slowly at first and then build the duet in speed and complexity.

Further Development

The dancers can share the original movement material so that one dancer starts and performs a set amount of counts and then the partner continues dancing the original phrase. You can also have them try it with more dancers. You could make a piece of a dance with duets that have moments of unison and moments that are unique as a section of the work.

Ghost

This improvisation is a great way to create more movement material for solo studies.

1. Ask the dancers to go over the phrase or sequence and to be aware of what levels, pathways and planes they move in.

2. Ask them to perform the first movement and remember where it moved in the space as if it made a trace like a light. Next, ask them to interact with the movement as if it has been filmed and played back to them in 3-D. So, they are dancing with and responding to themselves from a few seconds ago. For example, if the original movement was an arm to the side the response movement could be to duck under it.

3. Tell the dancer to interact with the ghost in the space; have him or her imagine another dancer demonstrating and then complement, contrast, move through spaces created, push, pull, lift, jump over or perform and so on. The dancer can choose any movements to express the relationship with the ghost.

4. Have dancers perform their movement responses to a partner and give each other feedback about what works and what can be changed.

Teaching Tip

If the dancers find this difficult to understand on their own they could first try it in pairs. One dancer could perform a phrase and the other can make a spontaneous response.

Further Development

Usually this task gives the movement material an artistic intension because the dancer's focus is directed towards the space that is implied. You can work with this concept further by asking the dancers to pause several times and trace the movement material of the original phrase with the eyes or head. They can also increase the speed of some movements so that they don't make contact with themselves in the original sequence.

Taking Away

This development is very simple but can be very effective. It can work with a duo or trio created from any of the improvisations in this book. It looks more effective if it includes lifts, contact moments or counterbalances.

Dancing a duet with a partner.

1. Ask the dancers to go over the duo or trio and think about the timing, effort, force and quality of their own movements within the dance.

2. If necessary or desired, have them change any of these ideas to make it feel more like a performance. At this point they can also show it to another group.

Dancing the same duet without a partner.

3. Next, ask one dancer to perform the duet but without the other dancer. Ask them to be true to the original movements and keep the qualities and dynamics that were in the original duo or trio.

Teaching Tip

The dancers may find performing without a partner a difficult concept to grasp. If you have a mature group of dancers who are open to trying new things you could get them to perform on their own in front of the other dancers without any practice. The audience can point out moments that are interesting to watch.

Further Development

If the dancers are choreographing a solo composition, this is a great way to get sequences of material and allows the dancers to work in pairs. You can also layer on narrative ideas to the solos such as loss, memories, longing, hopes or conflict, and as you watch the solos you can ask the audience of dancers what it meant to them. If you add on different styles of music you can create amazing narratives and emotional ideas.

Same but Different

This development asks the dancers to play with all the different ways that movements can change and develop. The dancers may discover new ways of editing movements that become part of their own choreographic style.

Two dancers with the same lower body action but different upper body.

1. Have dancers find a partner and face each other. One dancer performs the first few counts of the sequence. The partner then creates a short sequence that keeps some of the material the same but changes some of it either simply with choreographic devices (e.g., speed, force, facing, level, timing) or with completely new movement material joined into the sequence in several places.

2. Have them do this again. This time the first dancer responds by repeating something from the short phrase their partner just showed them and creating something different. Or, they can pick up the original phrase again.

3. Ask dancers to come up with more interesting themes to their responses. For example, the interaction could have a question and answer feel to it or, if dancing at the same time, dancers could travel around the space together facing the same way.

Teaching Tip

You could start this improvisation by showing movements yourself and having all the dancers respond at once in their own ways. You can repeat this development with any movements to get the dancers used to responding quickly. If you see a few good examples of dancers responding whilst keeping some essence of the original, then ask these dancers to demonstrate their work to the rest of the group. You can have dancers try this as an improvisation instead of using learnt material to let the dancers decide in the moment what their response may be.

Further Development

If the dancers are creating interesting movement material you may want to try it with a quartet. One dancer could lead the others with the original phrase or they could experiment with passing the phrase between them.

Retrograde

This development is a simple concept and it is one of the most effective. Choreographer Rafael Bonachela (Rambert Dance Company, Sydney Dance Company, Kylie Minogue Fever Tour) uses retrograde in most of his pieces to create unusual yet interesting movements. The dancers need a sequence to develop. If you want to make a small group piece it may add clarity to have the dancers use the same phrase.

Dancers all perform the same phrase backwards.

1. Ask the dancers to take a short section of their sequence and perform it whilst thinking about where the actions happen in the space around then.

2. Next, get them to perform this short excerpt backwards just as if it had been filmed and they are rewinding it.

3. Have the dancer play with moving forwards and backwards at any point in the phrase.

4. Ask the dancers to set when they go forwards, where and when they go backwards and what is repeated to create a new phrase.

Teaching Tip

You may want to try this development with a phrase that travels in a straight line. This way, you can get small groups of dancers to perform simultaneously from one side of the room.

Further Development

Watching phrases in reverse can often make movement material look interesting; you may end up not using the original phrase in the piece of choreography. Have dancers give each other feedback about which direction works best for the movements in the piece.

Intention Invention

In this development, dancers can perform any sequence or longer phrase and change the mood, atmosphere, intention, dynamic, quality, meaning or emotion. Depending on time and space limitations, you can have one dancer perform at a time or have small groups dance in unison.

Dancers explore different meanings behind the movement.

1. Begin with a phrase or sequence that the dancers know. Have dancers work alone or in pairs. Have them choose commands from the lists that follow to develop their work.

2. Have dancers perform their work. Add music to this performance. You can use various types of music with complex rhythms, time signatures, tempos and instruments, including voice. You may try different sound scores: found sound, sound made by other dancers—indeed anything.

Solo Task Choices

- Perform it as quickly as possible.
- Perform it as slowly as possible.

- Perform it as if the body were heavy (on the head, sinking).
- Perform it as if you needed the toilet.
- Perform it as if you were late for a train.
- Perform it as if you were sleepy.
- Perform it as if they were not happy to be watched.
- Perform it as if you were a super hero.
- Perform it as if you were a robot.
- Perform it as if they had two heavy suitcases.
- Perform it as if you were thirsty.
- Perform it as if you were dancing on stones or a hot surface.
- Perform it as if you were turning into a dog.
- Perform it as if you were under water or in custard.
- Perform it as if you had long limbs like an octopus.

Duet Task Choices

- One dancer must get in the way of another so that they have to find a way to dance over or under or move them out the way repeatedly.
- One dancer must try to get in front so that the audience cannot see the other.
- Perform the sequence as if dancer A were in love with dancer B.
- Perform the sequence as if dancer A were an aerobics instructor and dancer B were a member of the class.

Teaching Tip

Once the dancers have explored these choices they can also add verbal sounds or text to give the movements a physical theatre feel to them.

Further Development

You or the dancers can add suggestions to these lists.

A Recipe

This development is a step-by-step guide to making a whole dance composition. The first and only ingredient is a sequence created from an improvisation in this book or from a piece of professional repertoire. The longer the original sequence, the greater the scope of material that the dancers have to work with. This first phrase is phrase D. Do three things with it (this is development):

Step 1: On your own, create your own version of the phrase.

1. Pick your own favourite bits. They can be fragmented moments that you put back together in a new order so that they flow as one. Make it as long or as short as you like.

2. Change the facing and timing of at least two of these movements, and repeat one of the movements.

3. Teach your version to another dancer.

4. This version is phrase C.

Dancers make a duet with existing phrases.

Step 2: In pairs, make a travelling phrase.

1. Take five movements that you think could really travel and make them cover the dance space. You could run whilst doing an arm gesture, take a movement into a jump and even add a step pattern.

2. Next, try to make the phrase go into and out of the floor and change the direction that it travels; this may help you to make contact with your partner.

3. This is phrase B.

4. Next, explore crossing the space with your sequence and try to find moments in which you can make contact with your partner

or another two dancers. This could even be a jump with your hands on your partner to jump to the side, a lift or going under or over your partner as many times as you think you can make contact on your pathway.

5. Try playing with breaking it up so that one partner walks and watches for a few counts, then the other, then both dance in unison. Find one point at which to stop and look at each other; this could be a moment of stillness.

6. This is phrase A.

Step 3: In pairs or in trios, make the repertoire into a duet or trio.

1. Use the original phrase (D) and try to complement the movement material by filling in the spaces left as your partner moves. Switch roles so that the repertoire keeps going but is passed between the dancers.

2. Find two moments in which you can push or pull the other dancers into the next move within the phrase that has been created. Next, find two moments in which you can counterbalance or take another dancer's weight.

3. If you are making a quartet you will have two duets that can also be learnt by the other pair.

4. This can be phrase A2.

Step 4: Structure the whole dance composition.

1. The dancers in twos or threes will end up with one or two duets or a trio (A), the original sequence (D), two solo phrases (C) and a travelling phrase (B).

2. To make a whole dance composition you could make a simple Rondo structure: A, B, A2, C, A, D, A2. This is where the A phrase keeps coming back as a chorus would do in a song. You could also use any other phrase you created to be repeated throughout the piece. You could also find a chance way to order these small sections together (e.g., rolling a dice).

Teaching Tip

You can give this recipe to pairs as a handout. They can follow the instructions independently or you can lead them through each step.

Further Development

The dancers could create their own recipes to use themselves or to hand to other dancers.

Glossary

abstraction—An idea or concept conveyed through movement and removed from its original context.

accumulation—Building movements by adding them together (e.g., performing movement 1, then 1 and 2 and then 1, 2 and 3).

aerial steps—Actions that jump. There are five types of jumps: sauté, jeté, assemblé, sissonne and temps levé.

alignment—The relationship of the skeleton to the line of gravity and base of support.

amalgamation—Using two or more choreographic devices at once; can also be a sequence of dance movements that use different styles, body actions and timings.

aural setting—The sounds that accompany the dance: music, voice, natural sound and found sound.

balance—A state of equilibrium referring to the balance of weight or the spatial arrangement of bodies. Designs may be balanced on both sides of centre (symmetrical) or balanced off centre (asymmetrical).

binary—A dance composition consisting of two parts: AB.

body actions—The basic ways the body moves: flexion, extension, rotation, jumps, travelling, balance, stillness, gesture and turning.

canon—A passage, movement sequence or piece of music in which the parts are done in succession, overlapping one another (e.g., reverting, simultaneous, cumulative).

choreographic devices—Ways to manipulate movement material (repetition, retrograde, change of levels, change of planes, instrumentation, ornamentation, change of quality, change of force, change of rhythm, change of timing and speed, incorporative, inversion, change of staging, change of intention, change of facing, fragmentation, accumulation, use of canon, change of quality, change of background and amalgamation). There are 21 altogether.

choreography—Creation and composition of dances by arranging or inventing steps, movements and movement pattern.

collage—A compositional structure consisting of bits and pieces of assorted materials brought together to make a whole.

compositional structure—The way in which a dance is formed (e.g., binary, episodic, fugue and so on). The manner in which a dance is constructed or organised; a supporting framework or the essential parts of a dance (i.e., also called *dance structures* or *compositional form*).

constituent features—The parts that make up the whole piece of choreography (e.g., aural setting, physical setting, number of dancers, theme, the choreographic devices, the movement material and so on). They are all the things you would use in dance appreciation.

contrast—To emphasise differences; in dance, two movements that differ in energy, space (size, direction, level), design (symmetrical and asymmetrical, open and closed), timing (fast and slow, even and uneven), themes or patterns.

dance phrase—A partial dance idea composed of a series of connecting movements; similar to a sentence in the written form. It contains a beginning, a middle, an end and a high point.

dance sequence—Order in which a series of phrased movements and shape occurs.

dynamics—Energy of movement expressed in varying intensities, accent and quality.

facing—Where a dancer faces when performing each action (e.g., downstage, out to the audience, towards another dancer or a body part).

focus—In general, a gathering of forces to increase the projection of intent. In particular, it refers to a dancer's line of sight.

force or energy—The conversion of potential energy into kinetic energy; affects *quality* of movement. A dancer's energy reveals the effects of gravity on the body, is projected into space, and affects emotional and spatial relationships and intentions.

fragmentation—Using only part of a motif, isolating movements.

genre—A particular kind or style of dance, such as ballet, jazz, modern folk or tap.

gesture—Movement of a body part or combination of parts, with emphasis on its expressive characteristics, including movements of the body not supporting weight.

improvisation—Movement created spontaneously; can be freeform or highly structured environments, always including an element of chance.

incorporative—Adding new or incorporating different movements into a motif or phrase; a choreographic device.

instrumentation—To perform a movement with a different body part. A circle with the arm could become a rond de jambe or circle with the leg.

intension—The idea, emotion or theme behind the movement or dance.

inversion—Movement performed laterally or upside down.

isolated movement—Movement executed with one body part or a small part of the body. Examples include rolling the head, shrugging the shoulders and rotating the pelvis.

levels—Areas of space: low, middle and high.

locomotion or travelling—A form of physical movement progressing from one place to another. Basic locomotion movements include walking, running, galloping, jumping, hopping, skipping, sliding and leaping.

motif—Distinctive and recurring movements used to provide a theme or unifying idea.

musicality—A dancer's or choreographer's attention and responsiveness to musical elements.

ornamentation—Adding embellishment to movements (e.g., wiggle fingers, add loops or zigzags to pathways).

pathways—A line along which a person or part of the person, such as an arm or head, moves (e.g., her arm took a circular path, or he traveled along a zigzag pathway).

phrase—The smallest unit of form containing a beginning, middle and an end and a high point.

physical setting—The physical parts of the dance (e.g., costume, set, lighting and properties).

planes—Imaginary lines forming flat surfaces that intersect through the body; horizontal, vertical and sagittal.

principles of composition—The presence of unity, continuity (transitions) and variety (contrasts and repetition) in choreography.

projection—A confident presentation of one's body and energy to communicate movement and meaning clearly to an audience.

quality—The description of movements (e.g., sustained, percussive, suspended, swinging, quivery, fluid, jagged, collapsing).

release technique—A style of modern dance that explores gravity, the weight of the body, the natural ease of movement, energy, flow and even the pathways this takes through the body. This is a general term, although several schools of thought exist.

repetition—Duplication of a movement or movement's phrases within dance choreography.

retrograde—To reverse the order of a sequence of dance choreography.

rhythm—A structure of movement patterns in time; a movement with a regular succession of strong and weak elements; the pattern produced by emphasis and duration of notes in music.

rond de jambe—A French term meaning round of leg; an action where the leg draws a circular shape or pathway on the floor or in the air.

rondo—A dance piece in which a section is repeated throughout the dance; this is similar to a chorus in a song.

shape—A position of the body or group of bodies in space, such as curved, straight, angular, twisted, symmetrical, asymmetrical and so on.

shaping a dance—Considering the aspects of form and structure when constructing a piece of choreography.

space—The immediate spherical space surrounding the body in all directions. Use of space includes shape, direction, path, range and level of movement. Space is also the location of a performed dance.

staging—Where a dancer is on stage (e.g., up stage, down stage, stage left, stage right).

technique—The dancer's physical skills that enable him or her to execute the steps and movements required in different dances. Different styles, or genres of dance often have specific techniques.

tempo—The speed of music or a dance.

theme and variation—A compositional structure characterised by a theme of clear movement sequences that are used as a basic structure for different variations.

time—Involves rhythm, phrasing, tempo, accent and duration. Time can be metered as in music, or based on body rhythms such as breath, emotions and heartbeat.

transition—How one movement, phrase or section of a dance progresses into the next; a linking movement or idea.

unison—Identical dance movement that takes place at the same time in a group.

variety—A quantity or range of different things. To maintain audience interest, the choreographer must provide variety within the development of the dance. Contrasts in the use of space, force and spatial designs as well as some repetition of movements and motifs provide variety.

weight—A term that expresses quality of movement and literal force; it is often spoken about when considering how to give the body weight and take another person in a support of lift.

About the Author

Justine Reeve is a veteran dance teacher, having earned her BA (honors) in dance and related arts and postgraduate diploma in dance and collaborative arts from the University of Chichester in West Sussex, England, and a postgraduate certificate in education (PGCE). She is the artistic director of the West Sussex Youth Dance Company, an A-level dance examiner and a standards verifier for BTEC firsts and national diploma in dance.

Ms. Reeve has written units for the BTEC syllabus for 2007 and 2010 specifications and has delivered continued professional development courses for key stage 4 and 5 teachers of dance curriculum in the UK. She is also a visiting lecturer at the University of Chichester for undergraduate and master's students in education.

She has been the director of dance at the BRIT School, a dance animateur with Rambert Dance Company and a choreographer with her own company, the Puppik Dance Company. She enjoys visiting the theatre, reading and raising her young family.

You'll find other outstanding
dance resources at
www.HumanKinetics.com